ALSO BY
KATTY KAY, CLAIRE SHIPMAN, AND JILLELLYN RILEY

The Confidence Code for Girls

The Confidence Code for Girls Journal

LIVING THE CONFIDENCE CODE

KATTY KAY, CLAIRE SHIPMAN,
AND JILLELLYN RILEY

HARPER

An Imprint of HarperCollins*Publishers*

Library of Congress Control Number: 2020931677
ISBN 978-0-06-295411-4 — ISBN 978-0-06-299869-9 (special ed)

Typography by Michelle Gengaro-Kokmen
20 21 22 23 24 PC/LSCC 10 9 8 7 6 5 4 3 2 1
❖
First Edition

This is dedicated to the astonishing force
that is this generation of girls. Their power
and passion are inspirational and humbling.
We all have a lot to learn from them.

contents

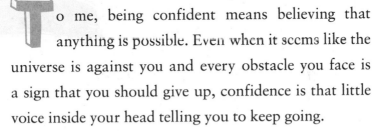

Foreword

To me, being confident means believing that anything is possible. Even when it seems like the universe is against you and every obstacle you face is a sign that you should give up, confidence is that little voice inside your head telling you to keep going.

And you're never too young to start listening to that voice. When I was five years old, my biggest dream was to go to the Olympics as a member of the United States gymnastics team. But I didn't keep that wish to myself, or think it was silly to be that ambitious.

What I did do was hear that voice inside me and decide to listen to it. I excitedly told my family about my Olympics dream, and they said, "Okay, we'll help you get there." That choice—to speak your truth instead of letting fear hold you back—is an important step in building confidence, no matter how old you are.

Which is why I'm so excited for you to read the book you're holding in your hands.

Living the Confidence Code is a collection of real stories from girls like you and me who are using their confidence to stay true to themselves, dismiss self-doubt, and achieve amazing things—whether it's trying to start a business, thrive with a disability, or become a political activist. Girls from around the world and a variety of backgrounds are here to share encouragement and their own special tips for creating confidence.

They've even inspired me to share a few of my own.

Find your cheering section. I was lucky to grow up with parents and siblings who took me seriously and supported my dreams. When I was training and eating healthy, they ate right and exercised to let me know they were fully behind me. You want people in your corner like that—cheerleaders who will *say* they believe in you and *show* it, too.

Dare to defy naysayers. Wherever you go, there will be cynics who will say and do discouraging things, but don't let them throw you off course. When I tried to compete at an international meet, someone told me I wouldn't qualify because it was too difficult. That same someone also told me that I'd never make Nationals or the Olympics. If I had let this person inside my head to mess with my confidence, I'd never be where I am today.

It's all about attitude. A few years ago, I suffered two serious injuries that derailed all my career plans. It was a huge setback and there were times when I wasn't sure I'd be able to return to the sport that I loved. When I began to compete again, I didn't focus on winning—I chose to simply be grateful to be living my dream. That change in mind-set gave me the inner strength to carry on and succeed. I wound up winning Nationals and going to the 2016 Olympics, where I won a silver medal for the balance beam, and Team USA won the gold!

My experiences might not be exactly like your experiences, but there's power in sharing our stories with each other. That's why a book like this is so important. Our lives aren't the same, but looking at this incredible group of girls, it's easy to see that listening to and learning from one another helps us become confident and strong.

I really hope you enjoy *Living the Confidence Code* as much as I did. Just turn the page to get started—and be inspired.

—**Laurie Hernandez**,
gold medal-winning Olympic gymnast
and bestselling author of *I Got This*

Introduction

You're about to meet some incredible girls. Some are brave and some are thoughtful; some are creative and some are studious; some are cautious and some are even rule-breaking. They all have cool stories and interesting things to say, and we think you will like them.

And you'll probably find a few who seem like you, or a few who care about the things you care about. Why are they here? They all managed to create the confidence to try something, to overcome something, to take some kind of action.

We all know what confidence feels like, right? Maybe it's that huge jolt of positive energy that lets us tackle something new or something hard? Or that rock-steady reassuring stream that sustains us like oxygen? When you read these stories, you will see that confidence looks and feels really different for different people, and that it's possible to have different paths to using and creating it.

Confidence can let you speak up when you are scared, try something unfamiliar when you might massively mess it up, or risk making everyone around you mad, if you don't do what people expect. These girls did all those things, and much more. And they have one thing in common: they figured out how to *build* the confidence to do what they want.

SO WHAT EXACTLY IS CONFIDENCE, ANYWAY?
THE SCIENTIFIC DEFINITION:

confidence is what turns our thoughts into action.

Thoughts + confidence = Action

Confidence helps you take a vague concept, a random thought floating around in your brain, and make it into a reality. (If you've read our other books, *The Confidence Code for Girls* and *The Confidence Code for Girls Journal*, you will be all over this!)

Without confidence, we'd never leave the coziness of our comfort zones and we'd certainly never try new or difficult things. One of the coolest things about confidence is that we all have some, but we can MAKE more. How? It's like an incredible loop.

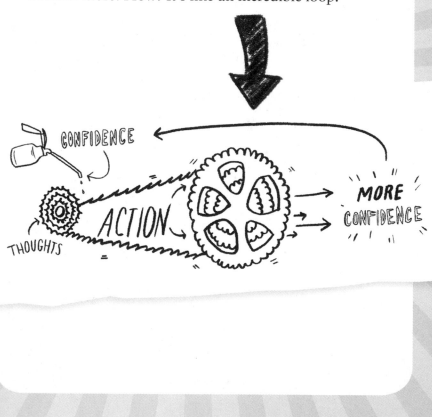

The more we risk and do things, the more confidence we make. Here's the basic recipe, which we call the **CONFIDENCE CODE**:

Risk more, think less, be yourself.

Risk More: Try, try, try. Try something that intimidates you, something that you've never done before or something that you feel strongly needs to be done. Take the risk. Even if you might fail.

Yep, we said it. Fail: the word that makes people quake. Taking risks means that you will fail because, at some point, everybody does. No getting around it. And it's not fun. But you can always dust yourself off and try again. Rebounding and being resilient—these will also help you build more confidence.

Think Less: Stop the negative voices in your head from warning you to stop, from telling you that you might fail. Those voices keep you from ACTING!

Be Yourself: This is the best place to find real confidence—inside your very best, most genuine, most authentic self. Don't be limited by trying to make everyone else happy, or by confining yourself to some version of fake perfection.

The more confidence you make, the more you can tackle the hard, scary, but ultimately most important stuff in your life. This may seem kind of nuts.

Risk? Fail? Stop worrying about what other people think?

But confidence works. It really does. It gives you the courage, the push, to get off the couch and do fun, exciting, and meaningful things.

We think the best way to understand confidence is to see it in action. These girls and their stories can show you all the different ways confidence can look and feel.

We weren't looking for perfect girls (they don't exist!). We were looking for girls who have really wrestled with building confidence, who have struggled and persisted, who have sometimes failed but kept going anyway, who have given up trying to be perfect and instead transformed their doubts and fears into action.

It wasn't easy, by the way, to pick a small group of girls. Girls everywhere have incredible stories, including you, no doubt. And girls have many different paths—some winding, some more straightforward—toward confidence.

For some girls, their actions are everyday things, close to home. For others, the action is about a bigger issue, one that touches a lot of people. Big or small or somewhere in-between—the scale may vary but the *process* of taking action is the same.

You may not agree with

everything these girls say or everything they do. That's OK. In the same situation, you might do the opposite, make a different choice or have a different reaction or come up with a different solution. That's OK, too.

It's really the doing—the building confidence—that matters. We hope their stories might trigger your own. Your story will be as unique as theirs are.

So read, think, check out the resources in the back of the book.

And then if you want, start to write your own!

Glossary/Key

Throughout the book, you are going to see girls trying, failing, and building their confidence. Notice the steps they take, the times they stumble, then when they brush themselves off and start again.

Check out this list of confidence building blocks and confidence pitfalls. We flagged some examples for you in the chapters with these handy-dandy symbols:

confidence Building Blocks

confidence Quicksand

But we certainly didn't mark every confidence tool or challenge, because we figured you'd start to recognize them on your own.

CONFIDENCE BUILDING BLOCKS

Risk ➔ Tackle something hard.

Failing ➔ Messing up means that you are human and that you tried. No shame there.

Rebounding ➔ Recover, even learn from trying and failing. It makes that confidence muscle stronger.

Resilience ➔ Hang in there, keep going even when you want to give up.

Authenticity ➔ Be the best, truest, most you version of you.

ME to WE ➔ Switching your thinking from yourself to other people can make you braver.

CONFIDENCE QUICKSAND

Fear ➔ Being scared to try, staying where you are comfortable, even if that holds you back from everything fun and exciting.

overthinking → Letting negative thoughts derail you from doing what you want.

Perfectionism → Attempting to achieve the impossible (nothing is perfect, ever) pulls you into a sticky trap that stops you from doing.

People-Pleasing → Worrying about what other people want or expect shuts down your own actions and shuts down you getting to be you.

Stereotyping → Being oppressed by assumptions and judgments people make about you, like your gender or ethnicity or any other aspect of who you are.

CHAPTER 1

Melati & Isabel Wijsen

Picture the island of Bali, one of the many volcanic islands in the archipelago of Indonesia. It's an idyllic place of gorgeous beaches and thriving coral reefs, ocean breezes, glistening blue water, and warm golden sunshine. It's the kind of place people dream of going on vacation. But for sisters Melati and Isabel, Bali is home. They have grown up with rice fields and sandy shores as their playground, in a house with open walls that has let them feel the beauty around them day and night.

But as they grew older, they started noticing an unnatural addition to their paradise. Heaps of plastic bags, everywhere—on the sides of roads, tripping them as they walked along the beach, and tangling around them when they went swimming. They were ten and twelve at the time, and they became disheartened, worried, and then angry as they learned more about the dangers of plastic for the environment. **Bye Bye Plastic Bags** was their answer.

Bye Bye Plastic Bags is doing exactly what the name says, loud and proud: it's an organization working to get rid of the single-use plastic bags that are choking oceans, rivers, and all kinds of marine habitats all over the world.

Scientists estimate that one hundred thousand marine animals are killed annually by plastic bags. And according to the Smithsonian Institute, plastic ends up in the bodies of about 700 different species.

You may have read the horrible stories about whales washing up with hundreds of pounds of shopping bags in their bellies. Or you may have seen the accounts of turtles starving because they mistake plastic for food, but then get no nourishment. Or fish, or crabs, or seals getting tangled up in the plastic mess and dying.

And guess what? The island of Bali is beautiful, but the country of Indonesia has been one of the worst plastic polluters *in the world*. Plus, the currents around these Indonesian islands tend to push even more plastic their way. Seeing this happen on their homeland motivated Melati and Isabel into action.

In the last five years, Bye Bye Plastic Bags, run by these two girls, has become a big deal in the fight against plastic pollution. They now have a team of people who help them. We asked them about the original spark for the movement and what made them think they could actually do something.

"Two things actually took place at the same time," Melati explains. "Imagine being ten and twelve. You're learning about all these incredible people throughout history, right? Hearing stories of Nelson Mandela, Lady Diana, Martin Luther King Jr. My sister and I went home all the time thinking, what can we do as kids, living on Bali? So while that was happening at school, we're walking around the island, along the river, or the ocean, or the rice fields, and there's plastic everywhere. We'd go swimming and it would wrap around our ankles. It was bad.

"So we kind of put these two ideas together. It's that beautiful, childlike feeling that the sky's not even the limit. Those exact words. We can go beyond the limit. It was the combination of the influence of people we admired and seeing with our own eyes what was wrong.

"At first, we didn't know what we were going to do, but we had pure passion and intention. We did some research on the internet and saw that forty other countries had banned plastic bags. And we thought, 'Well, if they can do it, we can do it, too.'"

The very first thing they did was start a petition online, calling for a ban. They rallied their friends, their parents, their friends' parents, their parents' friends, and anyone else they'd ever met to help push it out. Within the first twenty-four hours, they had about six thousand signatures.

They kept hitting Refresh . . . Refresh . . . Refresh to see more likes and more signatures. Who wouldn't? And the numbers kept going up by the hundreds, eventually thousands. They knew, without a doubt, that this plastic thing mattered, that it had power, and that other people cared.

"First we were just speaking to people we knew," Melati told us, "then we spoke at a school conference and then another school conference and then another. We organized some beach cleanups and did some community workshops. And slowly we realized we were building the idea to a movement, which could be this army of young people who wanted to make Bali plastic-bag-free."

But even an army of young people (*mostly* young people), as exciting as that was, could only get so far by speaking and cleaning up. To actually get *rid* of plastic bags on Bali, the sisters realized that they would have to change the law.

Changing laws isn't easy even for adults; for two young girls it's like moving a mountain. They had to wrap their minds around the legal processes, political procedures, regulations, and committees. And they didn't have a plan or a strategy or a budget to accomplish this. Even their mom was a little worried. They were, after all, kids. But Melati and Isabel knew that they needed to be creative in overcoming the obvious

CONFIDENCE QUICKSAND

Fear!

obstacles and think in ways that adults wouldn't be expecting.

In the meantime, though, their work was definitely getting noticed. Then they got invited to give their first international speech, in India, at a conference called INK Talk, which specializes in innovation and creative ways of taking action. It was a hugely exciting trip, plus a chance to visit the home of one of their idols, Mahatma Gandhi. And they got another idea. Gandhi was all about peaceful, nonviolent protest. One of his tools was a hunger strike. So the sisters went home to Bali and took to social media to announce their own hunger strike, promising to fast from dawn until dusk every day. Apparently, the idea of teenagers skipping meals was so persuasive that the governor of Bali agreed to meet with them right away.

CONFIDENCE
BUILDING
BLOCK

Resilience!

Although it was a positive meeting, things didn't change immediately (things rarely do!). It took Melati and Isabel years, in fact. The sisters kept at their antiplastic crusade, doing the fun and not-so-fun stuff that has to be done, all the while going to school, hitting the mall, and lazing around the beach with their friends, watching the sunset. At the same time, working for change.

Five years after they started the campaign, the law did change: single-use plastic bags have now been banned on the island of Bali. And the government of Indonesia has also pledged to reduce plastic pollution by 70 percent in the next five years.

Even though these sisters may seem like they've got everything figured out, they were quick to tell us that there are plenty of things that give them the creeps and make them want to hide under the bed. Melati is afraid of flying, especially by herself. She still gets nervous about speaking to kids her own age. Isabel actually loves being onstage and talking to groups, but she's superstitious about crossing the street. So it's not all a walk in the park—or a stroll on the beach—for them.

The importance of protecting the earth's water comes up again later in the book, in Autumn's story!

Of course, there are some folks resisting the plastic ban and all the changes it can bring, so

Melati and Isabel are still at work, calling out for signatures on Instagram and rallying their army to continue their work. As they say,

"The oceans are rising and so are we!"

Just Asking

What's your favorite comfort food that makes everything better?

Melati: Nasi campur (Indonesian dish with rice, tofu, lots of vegetables, and spices)
Isabel: Pizza and popcorn

What's the one thing that you couldn't live without?

Melati: My family   Isabel: My friends

If you were an animal, what would you be?

Melati: A turtle   Isabel: An elephant

What's the one place you've always wanted to go—your dream destination?

Melati: Africa   Isabel: Peru

What or who always makes you laugh?

Melati: My sister
Isabel: (back at you, sis!) My sister

What do you like to do on a lazy day?

Melati: Lie out in the sunshine
Isabel: Fall asleep while listening to music

CHAPTER 2

Riley Morrison

Dear Stephen Curry,

My name is Riley (just like your daughter ),
I'm 9 years old from Napa, California. I am a big
fan of yours. I enjoy going to Warriors games with
my dad. I asked my dad to buy me the new Curry
5s because I am starting a new basketball season.
My dad and I visited the Under Armour website and
were disappointed to see that there were no Curry 5s
for sale under the girls' section. However, they did
have them for sale under the boys' section, even to
customize. I know you support girl athletes because

you have two daughters and you host an all-girls basketball camp. I hope you can work with Under Armour to change this because girls want to rock the Curry 5s, too.

Sincerely,
Riley Morrison

Riley's letter pretty much says it all. In the fall of fourth grade, Riley was looking forward to being the point guard on her team in the upcoming season. To play her best, she wanted to start with new kicks from her favorite player, Golden State Warrior Steph Curry, also a point guard, and an NBA champion, All-Star, and MVP. She always wore his jersey (number 30) when she watched his games, whether at home or at the Oracle Arena in Oakland, California.

She felt like she could just tell that he's a great person: "I like that Steph's funny and he's kind and, to me, he's the best player in the world." She was also inspired by the way he handles the ball and the good choices he makes, so it made total sense to step out on the court in his shoes. Until she tried to buy them.

Riley and her dad both *love* sneakers, but when they

went shopping on the Under Armour website to check out the new shoes from Steph Curry, there was nothing on the girls page. Not one Curry. At first, she thought maybe they didn't make them in kids' sizes, but when she checked back a few weeks later, still no Curry 5s listed on the girls' page. Her dad clicked around and found plenty for sale on the boys' page.

What?! Riley didn't get angry, but she didn't think that was fair. As she says, "You might be a boy, you might be a girl, but boys still can wear pink, and girls still can wear blue. Because there's no difference. Just because you're a girl doesn't mean you don't like the Currys or want to have the Currys. Girls don't just want shoes in pink or purple. And girls like basketball, too." Riley knew she could just order the boys' shoes, but it frustrated her that they weren't marketing the Currys to girls. When they're not on the site or in the store specifically aimed at girls, it's like the company is saying, "You don't matter to us."

It wasn't the only time Riley had experienced this kind of frustration. When she tried to buy compression pants to wear for sports, for example, she could only find them in the boys' section. Usually, she would think, *"Whatever."* She's been into basketball since she was four and nothing's going to stop her from loving the game. But at the same time, she didn't like the message it sent—that girls didn't really need sports clothes, or were not expected to wear them. "Well," she told us, "maybe back in the day, girls didn't have as many rights as men. But not anymore!"

Looking around at the pictures on the wall in the girls' sections at stores, or online, or even seeing female athletes on TV, Riley had also noticed that they get a ton of attention for their appearance, rather than what they do. She told us, "It's about their hair, and their dresses, and their makeup. And it's never about their sport, always about how they look. I want to play for the WNBA, so when I'm interviewed I will say

'Ask me about what I'm doing, ask about the game, ask about my points or my shots. Don't ask me about what I'm wearing or what I look like.'"

Riley has a lot of feelings and opinions, but speaking up and using her voice isn't easy for her. Sometimes, like when she beat the fastest boy in a race only to be taunted that he'd let her win because she's a girl, Riley takes the high road and simply walks away. Even though she's comfortable and confident on the court, she can be really shy and quiet at school. And she'd already had one epic fail.

Earlier that fall, Riley ran for student council. She liked the idea of coming up with themes for assemblies and cool ideas for spirit days. It sounded fun and she felt like it would be good for her to take the risk, to push her-self out of the comfort zone of playing sports and into another kind of adventure. To run, she had to pitch herself in a letter to her fellow students, explaining why she should be elected. Her letter talked about her team leadership abilities, her hard work and dedication in sports, her passion to play the cello beautifully, and her desire to be braver off the basketball court or soccer field. She really liked what she wrote.

But she lost. Lost to someone who was a friend. Lost in front of the whole school. It was awful—this was nothing like losing a shot, a goal, or even a game, because she couldn't brush it

Turns out, Riley decided to run for student council because she was inspired by a book she'd just read: *The Confidence Code for Girls!*

CONFIDENCE BUILDING BLOCK

Failing!

off and go back out there. This time, the loss seemed permanent. When her dad picked her up from school, she couldn't hold it in. She just broke down, with heavy-duty sobbing and total despair. Why even try? Some kids were mean about it, she quit talking to the friend who won, and things seemed really rough.

All she had to cheer her up was the new basketball season, and those new Currys her dad had promised her. Maybe that's why she was able to take a risk and write that letter to her favorite player. Or maybe it was because she'd already experienced a painful failure and she knew she could get through it. But after looking at that website, something clicked.

She decided that Steph Curry must not know his brand didn't include girls' shoes, and she decided to be the one to tell him. Writing to a basketball legend about shoes, though, was bigger than one pair of sneakers for one single girl. For Riley, it was about making sure that girls like her, girls who love basketball, have the same cool opportunities as boys. Maybe that's why she felt like she COULD use her voice. It wasn't all about her; it was about other girls, too.

Riley thought about the biggest risk, the worst-case

scenario. Steph Curry might never see the letter. OK. Nothing might change. OK. Having already survived the student council catastrophe, Riley knew she could handle it.

She figured out exactly what she wanted to say to her hero, and she put it down on paper with kindness and respect. She says, "You don't have to be rude or angry to make a point." She sent it, and then her dad took her carefully worded letter and tweeted it out into the world.

A sports journalist, Liz Plank, supported her by tweeting it to all her followers. And with the incredible speed of a viral message, her voice reached Steph Curry, and he *did* answer. Right away! He answered Riley with his own handwritten note and posted it on his social media. Telling her that they would correct the problem, he also said, "Appreciate your helping us get better. We got you Riley! #moretocome"

She was in shock. Not only did Under Armour correct the problem, but Riley was invited to *codesign* a pair of Currys in honor of International Women's Day, March 8. Can you even imagine?! The money made by these shoes went toward a Curry Foundation college scholarship for a girl from the Bay Area. Riley's head was spinning—she helped make that happen!

Within just a few weeks of writing her letter, Riley had to work under a crazy-tight deadline to create the message for a sock liner inside the newest shoes. She brainstormed a couple of ideas, including an image of a letter like hers flying out of an envelope, before coming up with the best one: two girl ballers, dribbling and shooting, encircled by these words of encouragement: "Be Bold," "Girl Power," "Be Courageous," "Fearless," "Girls Hoop Too," and "Way to Make a Change."

According to *Forbes'* 2018 list of highest-paid athletes, there were no women in the top 100. Plus, NBA players make 100 times more than the women in the WNBA!

When she's older, Riley hopes to be a WNBA player and help make the women's league as big, popular, and well paid as the NBA. She also plans to be an author. Whatever happens, she told us that

"I can do more. I'm braver, I'm more confident. And I can use my voice for other things now."

JUST Asking

What's your favorite comfort food that makes everything better?

Watermelon and mac and cheese

What's the one thing that you couldn't live without?

My blanket that I've had forever!

If you were an animal, what would you be?

An elephant

What's the one place you've always wanted to go—your dream destination?

Spain

What or who always makes you laugh?

My dad

What do you like to do on a lazy day?

Watch my favorite YouTube channel

CHAPTER 3

Mari Copeny

ari will never forget what she started to see coming out of her faucets when she was eight years old: brown, smelly water, causing people's eyes to burn, skin to break out, hair to fall out—and also causing them to get really, really sick, sometimes with dangerous conditions like anemia or Legionnaires' disease. The water system in her hometown of Flint, Michigan, had become contaminated with high levels of bacteria and lead. The city had switched from Lake Huron to the Flint River for its water and hadn't purified it enough.

Some of the bacteria was especially nasty, like E. coli, which is a kind of bacteria that may live in your poop

We learned from the Environmental Defense Fund that about 10 million homes get water from lead pipes, and that lead can seep into the water. In Flint, thousands of kids have been exposed to lead.

but should never be in your drinking water. But the most serious was the lead. Exposure to lead can cause learning and developmental disabilities in kids, which meant that all over Flint, children were at risk.

To limit their exposure to this toxic water, Mari and her family (and lots of other people) were taking two-minute showers, buying bottled water, and desperately hoping for help from the government. Mari was overwhelmed, especially watching her little sister suffer. "The worst part of the water crisis," she told us, "was having to see my little sister hurting from the really bad rashes the water was giving her. She was so little and she would cry and she hated having to get the special ointment on her to try to help heal it."

Mari has never been afraid of the spotlight. She's competed in pageants, earning the title Little Miss Flint, and felt like she should get involved in the most urgent issues around her. So she tried to improve the relationship between the police and her community in Flint and worked at the food bank with her grand-mother. It's just who she is. Then when that disgusting, stinky, toxic water just kept coming out of the pipes, Mari wasn't going to sit around and wait for someone else to fix it. "When the water crisis happened," she told us, "I wanted to be a voice for the kids here, to fight for them. I hoped someone would listen to me."

When the federal govern-ment announced hearings in Congress about the water prob-lems in Flint, she and her family decided to head to Washington, DC. "I was excited and hoped that if we were going all the way to DC that maybe the president would come or send his wife to give the people coming some hope.

Later in the book, you will read about another girl, Gitanjali, who's also working to stop the lead-in-water problem!

"I didn't think anything would happen, but I wanted to at least try."

And try she did. Mari decided to write to President Barack Obama and ask for a meeting:

Mr. President,

Hello, my name is Mari Copeny and I'm 8 years old, I live in Flint, Michigan, and I'm more commonly known around town as "Little Miss Flint." I am one of the children that is affected by this water, and I've been doing my best to march in protest and to speak out for all the kids that live here in Flint. This Thursday I will be riding a bus to Washington, DC, to watch the congressional hearings of our governor, Rick Snyder. I know this is probably an odd request but I would love for a chance to meet you or your wife. My mom said chances are you will be too busy with more important things, but there is a lot of people coming on these buses and even just a meeting from you or your wife would really lift people's spirits. Thank you for all that you do for our country. I look forward to being able to come to Washington and to be able to see Gov. Snyder in person and to be able to be in the city where you live.

Thank You
Mari Copeny

Sometimes it's easy to think a bold step can feel overwhelming, or even silly. Mari knows that. Would her letter reach the president of the United States? She wasn't sure. "There is always a risk that people will not listen to me because I am a kid and some people don't believe that kids can have their own opinions on things."

Odd request or not, President Obama ended up coming to Flint! He wrote her back first, though, telling Mari, "You are right that presidents are often busy, but the truth is, in America, there is no more important title than citizen. And I am so proud of you for using your voice to speak out on behalf of the children of Flint." Decked out in her Little Miss Flint sash, she met the president the next month and said to him, "You know, I wrote to you!" He laughed and said, "I know! That's why I decided to come."

We asked her how it felt when she got through to the president of the United States. Mari, now eleven years old, says, "That's when I knew I was in a position to be able to do as much as possible now that more people were learning about who I was."

And was that scary for Mari? "It wasn't intimidating to me," she remembers, "but it was intimidating to my mom. She didn't think that anyone would listen to a kid, let alone a kid out in the middle of winter in the cold. I knew whether people listened to me or not, I still needed to fight."

Meeting President Obama turned out to be just the first step, fueling her confidence to keep doing what she believes in. And what does confidence mean to Mari?

"Confidence to me is being able to wake up each day and tackle it with my head held high. When things get tough, to know that I can work through them, and when I need help, to know that help is there. It's knowing that I will always be who I am and that nobody can take that from me."

You might think confidence comes easily to Mari, but it doesn't always, just as it doesn't for the rest of us. She says we'd be surprised about what scares her and what doesn't. "When I'm around kids I don't know for the first time I get really shy, not knowing if they will like me or not." But Mari says she's learned to just keep going, whether or not she's scared.

CONFIDENCE QUICKSAND

Fear!

"This year I was terrified to try out to play basketball, but my friends were doing it, so I just did it. I learned a lot and now am getting better and better at it. That first game I was so scared I didn't even move, but now I actually play. At one point I wanted to quit, but I didn't. I just forced myself to do it, even if I'm scared. It's easier to just do it than to think about it—listening to the coach and learning at practices and from my teammates. **The hardest part is taking that first step.** Once you start, though, it will be so much easier, and you will feel silly for even being afraid to take that first step."

Her biggest challenge, most of the time? Her own thoughts. "Sometimes I can get caught in negative thoughts," she says, "because some of the things I want to achieve seem impossible."

CONFIDENCE QUICKSAND

overthinking!

The water situation in Flint, for example, is better, but the problem has not gone away. Many people still have to use bottled water. Mari is also trying to build community spirit while this work for clean water goes on. After organizing free screenings of cool movies like *Black Panther* and *A Wrinkle in Time*, she's started the

Dear Flint Kids Project on Twitter, a letter-writing campaign for people all over the country to share happy and uplifting messages with kids in Flint.

Mari also takes great comfort in finding allies to help her. "I have my family," she explains, "especially my mom, who always has my back. I have so many role models, but one in particular is Bernice King (Dr. Martin Luther King's daughter and civil rights activist). She is one that always reminds me that I am a light and to let that light shine no matter what."

Just Asking

What's your favorite comfort food that makes everything better?

Bacon

What's the one thing that you couldn't live without?

A pencil and paper

If you were an animal, what would you be?

A jellyfish

What's the one place you've always wanted to go—your dream destination?

Japan

What or who always makes you laugh?

Myself

What do you like to do on a lazy day?

Sleep

CHAPTER 4

Ciara-Beth Griffin

As a little girl, Ciara-Beth found adults hard to understand sometimes. Of course, most kids are baffled by grown-ups (it's not easy to see what's so appealing about rules and chores and bedtimes and broccoli), but for Ciara-Beth, there was more to it. She'd known she was unique from the moment she started preschool—she took in information differently, which meant that when she tried to line up her version of things with everyone else's, it didn't always match up. Sometimes Ciara-Beth felt like she was swimming through pudding.

Here's an example: Ciara-Beth lives on the west

coast of Ireland near the city of Galway, which gets a ton of rain. So when someone would make a comment like "It's raining cats and dogs today," Ciara-Beth expected to see soaking-wet, confused animals pelting down from the sky. She just didn't react like typical kids, almost ever.

After a school fire drill when she was six, she became fixated on fires for months and couldn't let anyone in her family sleep until she'd checked and rechecked all the switches in their house. Or she worried about the potential for an explosive car crash on the short ride to school, even though most vehicles in her rural village were lumbering tractors moving with all the speed of turtles. So when she was diagnosed with autism at thirteen, it was actually a relief, a confirmation of what she'd realized all along.

Her brain *does* process things differently; it's not something she's

According to the organization Autistic Advocacy, autism is also called a neurodiversity disorder, which means that the brain processes language, sights, sounds, and other information differently. People use the phrase "on the spectrum" because there are many different shades of autism. It can be mild or extreme.

making up. As she says, "If you're going from A to Z, there's a conventional route in your brain where you go from A, B, C, D, and all the way through to Z. But my brain would seem to go from A to Q and then back to C, and it would take a much more scenic route." Far from being embarrassed, Ciara-Beth and her family were grateful for the diagnosis because it brought a new understanding about the way her brain works.

You will read about Greta, another girl with autism, later in the book and how she also uses it to help her with her mission! And you will also meet Angelina, who has faced similar hurdles because of the way her brain processes information.

Once she started getting the extra help and services she needed, she had a new mission: helping other people with autism. Her first move? Designing an app to practice a seemingly simple, but important, skill—making eye contact.

It's such an easy thing to take for granted, looking people in the eye. Ciara-Beth had struggled with eye contact herself, like lots of people with autism. How much have you ever thought about it? A steady gaze that meets someone else straight in the eye sends the message that you're listening and have nothing to hide. If you avoid eye contact with your teachers, they automatically think you are guilty of something, right? But what happens if meeting someone's eyes is hard for you? What happens if you just can't do it?

For Ciara-Beth, the consequences of avoiding eye contact were some of the many issues she discovered when she found out she had autism.

"After my diagnosis, I jumped into a pile of academic research. I read every single article I could find online about how my brain works, why it works that way, and how many people were like me. I found some pretty scary statistics. Right now, 85 percent of the people who have autism in Ireland are completely unemployed. And then I found another statistic that said that 67 percent of employers feel like failure to make eye contact in an interview means you're at a disadvantage and it could potentially cost you a job. By the time I was in middle school, I could only talk to a handful of people and look them in the eye. And it did obviously cost me friends, because it's quite frustrating to be friends with a person who's sitting right there in front of you but won't talk or look at you.

"Learning that autism is frequently associated with the failure to make eye contact, I was like, well, obvious problem here. We're being unknowingly discriminated against in these situations, probably unintentionally. And I thought: I can fix this."

Although she'd never even tried to turn on a computer (they intimidated her), she decided that an app would help people develop and practice that skill, at home, on their own terms, where it wouldn't seem intimidating. It would be easier than trying it in a doctor's or therapist's office. Plus, as she knew from her research, the wait for doctors who can diagnose autism in Ireland's national health service can take two years, with an even longer wait for specialists like occupational or speech therapists. Her app could help people faster than that. She felt confident about her concept; now she needed to make it a reality.

She figured out how to get a grant from a family research center in Galway to help her develop a prototype to compete in a science fair. She started by googling and youtubing nonstop.

CONFIDENCE BUILDING BLOCK

Risk!

She'd never studied coding, and sometimes felt in over her head, but she loved to learn. She'd find some code, take it apart, and then try to put it back together like a jigsaw, puzzling out which bits did what. Sometimes, the result wound up being more like a piecemeal Frankenstein monster than what she wanted, but then she'd scrap it and try again. Her extensive childhood experience with Legos paid off!

She also didn't hesitate to seek help, even though that was incredibly hard for her, too. Friends of friends, acquaintances of acquaintances, people who knew other people thrice removed, even a start-up game design company—she wasn't shy about pushing them for advice or practical tips to create her vision.

Once she got all this help, she ended up competing all over the place, in the biggest science fairs in Ireland, the UNESCO Youth Forum in Paris, and summits in New York City and Switzerland. It took a couple of years, and it was definitely a long, totally frustrating road. The more she traveled and talked about it, though, the more she realized how many people needed and wanted this kind of help. Her kind of help. Everywhere she went, she told us, "there were a lot of people who

50

said, 'This will be so helpful for my cousin or my brother or my uncle or my friend.'"

Finally, the app **MiContact** was launched in the spring of 2019, with hundreds of people using it right away. MiContact works like a matching game, with pictures of faces whose eyes have little shapes inside them, like moons or triangles, and then you click on the matching shape at the bottom of the screen. It gets people with autism used to looking directly at people's eyes, on a screen to start, which begins to build that habit and make it less frightening in real life. Ciara-Beth is proud that it's out in the world, that it's not a thing just in her head anymore. And she wants to do more. She's planning to create a website called Amazingly Autistic that will be an online digital library of tools and resources.

In sharing what she calls her "superhero origin story," Ciara-Beth is the first to say that none of this was easy. According to her, most of the time she was constantly haunted by how "royally" she could mess it up.

"There was not a single element of MiContact that came naturally to me. There wasn't a single step where I was sure that what I was doing was right or good or even worth doing. There was just something in me that said **we have to do it**. And the more I thought about it, and the further I got, the more stubborn I got. I felt like I did not come this far to **only** come this far. I have to finish this."

But she tried to take the focus off herself and put it on how much the app could help others. When she started the MiContact project, she hated speaking to people in groups. It's still hard for her to wrap her head around her role as an advocate, talking to strangers about inclusion and diversity. She struggles with doubt, insecurities, and with a crippling case of perfectionism.

CONFIDENCE
QUICKSAND

Perfectionism!

"I'm still trying to learn that it's OK sometimes to submit an assignment before it's absolutely perfect. It's OK to do well and not get 100 percent. Not getting 100 percent isn't the end of the world. Most parents put pressure on their kids to do well in school; my parents have to stop me putting pressure on myself.

"You just get taken over by the What if I fail? What will other people think? And the nasty perfectionist voice in your head being very much like, 'Well, I'm not going to do it until I know I can do it perfectly.' Absolutely the wrong attitude to have because it's just not the way the human body works. We can't be perfect. It is physically impossible. So I'm trying to reason with that inner voice: 'Yeah, but there's no chance of it being perfect, so let's actually try.' I have to constantly say, 'Knock it off!'"

She's learned to quiet her inner critic, and to use outside discouraging criticism as fuel. Once, a man in a professional meeting about her app told her that she'd never do it. "He said I was a girl," she remembers, "I was young, and I had autism. What was I thinking? No way could I succeed, according to him. That made me mad. There were all of these things about me that I couldn't change. Not my age. Not the fact that I was autistic. Not the fact I was a girl. One reason this project got done is out of spite to those kind of people. Because a lot of the time, actually, it's because I'm young and because I'm a girl and because I'm autistic that I can do these things."

CONFIDENCE QUICKSAND

Stereotyping!

Other kinds of motivation are just as important in keeping her from giving up in the long run. "I have to reconnect myself to the main reason: I'm not doing this because it's easy. I'm doing it because it's important, it matters, and nobody else will do it if I don't." And she still has plenty of conversations with herself, but not the perfectionistic kind.

"The minute I think I can't do something, I check a note I wrote myself on my phone to look at in moments of doubt or panic. It says, *You didn't think you could do MiContact and that happened. You didn't think you'd do half a million other things that you've also done.*

"So if you don't think you can, the reality is you probably can."

Just Asking

What's your favorite comfort food that makes everything better?

French fries and vanilla shakes

What's the one thing that you couldn't live without?

Music and Legos

If you were an animal, what would you be?

A puppy, excitable and energetic

What's the one place you've always wanted to go—your dream destination?

New York City

What or who always makes you laugh?

My cat and my dog

What do you like to do on a lazy day?

Have a laid-back day with no plans. Comfy clothes, nice snacks, and chilling out.

CHAPTER 5

Haven Shepherd

Growing up in Missouri with her six athletic brothers and sisters, Haven knew she'd also be an athlete. Her family was always racing around following so many sports schedules that she spent most of her first ten years practically living at baseball parks in the spring and summer, basketball courts in the winter, and volleyball practice the rest of the time. She figured when she was old enough, it would be her turn, too. The fact that she'd lost both her legs below the knee as an infant just didn't strike her as anything that would get in her way, not at all.

Haven was born in Vietnam. She was injured in a

bombing when she was tiny, which cost Haven her legs and her parents their lives. Since she was just a baby when it happened, Haven doesn't remember anything about that tragic day. She also doesn't remember the day her new parents, who'd traveled a thousand miles, came to her village to meet her, except that she believes it's all part of God's plan. Haven survived the explosion that killed her parents and was united with her true family, which she feels was God's purpose all along.

The Shepherds adopted her, and she was always treated like all the other kids in the family. Her parents never made her feel that there was anything she couldn't do. "One rule for everybody in our family," Haven says, "is that no one is a victim, and no one gets to feel sorry for themselves."

Haven feels like she was always just a regular girl, chasing other kids, throwing frogs at them on the playground or riding dirt bikes and four-wheelers around the broad countryside in southwest Missouri. Maybe she didn't run around exactly like everyone else, because she literally ran around on her nubs—that's what she calls the ends of her legs—and she tended to pull the knobs off kitchen cabinets when she needed to get up to the counter to reach the toaster, but she definitely didn't feel disadvantaged in any way. And when she wore her black, high-tech prosthetic legs, she says, "Everybody thought my legs were cool because I'm like a Transformer." Somehow, she says, "I was never afraid to be different because I always knew who I was and I loved that about myself. I'm Asian and I don't have legs and I can't take off my plastic legs to lie down during nap time in kindergarten. So what?"

Authenticity!

Haven's faith, combined with her family's support, allowed her to believe in herself, to believe that she could do anything, so she never doubted she'd also be an athlete. When it came time to find her sport, Haven first tried track. She'd never seen amputee athletes, so she remembers the spark she felt when she watched runners using high-tech prosthetic legs on TV, like the ones competitors use for the Paralympics. But those

Para athletics started from a group of World War II veterans and now includes thousands of people across the world, in many sports with many different abilities. Since 1960, the Paralympics have been held alongside the Olympics, every four years.

are expensive. Haven and her mom were eventually able to get a pair with a grant from a foundation, and Haven was determined to try her best at running. "My dad said you can't start something and not finish it," she told us, "so I always work hard to try and try until I do!"

CONFIDENCE BUILDING BLOCK

Resilience!

But she never fell in love with track. She did try, but as she says, "If it turns out that every time you do your sport, you start to cry, it's probably not for you." To encourage her to keep going, her parents sent her to a huge event in Oklahoma for young Para athletes that had all kinds of sports, like track, swimming, archery, and tennis. For the first time, she saw other athletes who looked more like her, and it was exciting. "This is a great community," she thought immediately, "this is a great place to show who you truly are." Plus, the passion all the kids brought to what they did was contagious.

At the same time, Haven realized that as hard as she tried (and as much as she cried), track was still not doing it for her. She needed to find *her* passion. She'd been swimming in her family's big backyard pool since she was tiny and loved paddling around, even though she didn't know exactly how to execute the right strokes, so she signed up for a swimming clinic. Immediately, she felt at home in the water. It's one of the places where she doesn't need her prosthetics at all. And it turns out, she was really good.

Haven remembers it as an almost blissful experience: "I felt completely free." She also savored the solitude of swimming; it gave her some time to be alone with her thoughts, to get to just be in her own head. "It teaches you a lot about yourself. Kids don't get to daydream anymore, because they watch YouTube instead," she said to us. "So swimming is an escape from the outside world while you are dedicating yourself to what you're doing."

Then, at her very first swim meet, she met Jessica Long, a Paralympic swimmer with thirteen gold medals, who is also a double amputee, exactly like Haven. Even better, Jessica seemed to understand just how nervous and scared Haven was, so she was incredibly kind. In addition to having to compete for the fastest time, Haven explains, "Swimming's a very intimate sport and you're in a little one-piece swimsuit in front of a bunch of people staring at your body. I wasn't very comfortable in the beginning because I was just used to swimming with my sisters in the summer." After Haven's event at that first meet, Jessica waited at the end of the pool with Haven's towel, and in that moment Haven knew: "This is totally where I belong." It might not have been her first sport, but it became The Sport.

At only twelve years old, she qualified for the Paralympics Emerging Swim Team and moved up competitive levels (from the bronze level to the gold level) quickly. After a few years, she started training full-time. By then, she didn't care if people were staring at her. "It's a good experience for everybody to see the side of me that's usually covered up by my prosthetics. That's what I really love about being an amputee; I get to teach my friends about this super-cool community."

In making this commitment to swimming, Haven has had to make other big choices. She's got an intense, heavy-duty training schedule at a swim club about a half hour from her house to keep up with all the competitions, and she travels around the country with the Challenged Athletes Foundation to raise awareness of people with physical challenges living active lives.

Trying to fit all of that into a regular school day was

impossible, so she and her mom decided when she was in eighth grade that she'd be homeschooled. Getting up at four a.m. for training, long hours in the pool, missing family events because of meets and travel—all of this with an eye toward the Paralympics in Tokyo in 2020—puts a lot of pressure on Haven. She relies on her brothers, sisters, and parents to help her keep from getting overwhelmed, as well as her faith in God.

For Haven, many angels and little miracles have happened to allow her to pursue her swimming passion. Many times money was super tight and it didn't look like she and her mom could afford the airfare or hotels or meals. But every time the situation was bleak, a generous donor stepped up unexpectedly and paid her expenses. Different versions of this happen all the time, making Haven feel that she's right to trust in God. She's been able to take risks, to try and sometimes fail, and to build her confidence with this deep well of faith to support her.

Now sixteen, Haven knows she's making significant sacrifices to be a swimmer. She definitely misses the excitement of back-to-school shopping, the inside jokes and fun times with friends in the hallways, and the glamour of prom. She also misses the comfort of nightly dinners at home or more time with her expansive family. She did recently get her driver's license and a new car, which she can drive with her prosthetic legs. This also means she can see her friends and be more independent. And she knows that her life will be about more than swimming, that she's got many more layers to her, but that right now, swimming is how she's learning about all those layers.

What does confidence mean to Haven?

"confidence is very much a state of mind and a choice.

"You know, I could be insecure because I don't have legs and feel sorry for myself all the time, or I could be confident and wear short shorts to show off my shiny black legs. If people stare at me, I can choose to think, 'Oh, you're staring at my legs,' or 'Oh, you think my jean jacket with twenty pounds of Disney World pins is cool.' I think confidence is choosing that one, choosing the best."

Just Asking

What's your favorite comfort food that makes everything better?

Steak

What's the one thing that you couldn't live without?

My family, but if it has to be a "thing," then moisturizer

If you were an animal, what would you be?

A bumblebee

What's the one place you've always wanted to go—your dream destination?

Paris or South Africa

What or who always makes you laugh?

My sister Haley

What do you like to do on a lazy day?

Sleep in, drink coffee, eat fried rice, do a face mask, and watch *Avatar* or *Man on Fire*

CHAPTER 6

Afghan Dreamers

The Afghan Dreamers is the perfect name for this robotics team of six girls, because nobody thought an all-girl team from Afghanistan was actually possible. And it almost didn't happen. Many girls in Afghanistan don't even go to school, much less know anything about robotics. An extremist religious group, the Taliban, ran the country for years, and they didn't think girls should be educated. They were very violent, severely punishing people who didn't follow their strict, rigid codes. The Taliban is no longer in power, but there is still a lot of conflict and poverty in the beautiful, mountainous country. A terrorist group called ISIS is still active. And girls' opportunities have been stifled for a long time. So when the Digital Citizen Fund, a group helping girls and women all over the world learn about tech, decided to form a team, it was hard.

Still, when the girls of the Afghan Dreamers heard about the auditions, they knew it was an opportunity to show what girls can achieve and to represent the best of their country. They rushed to try out, even though for them, risk and failure have far scarier consequences than for most of us—they risked getting physically attacked or even killed by people who still support the Taliban. But the strategies they used to face those risks, that possibility of failure? Universal. The same as any of you would use!

And it's worked! Now the Dreamers are role models for other girls, leading workshops on robotics and even helping to plan a new STEM school in Kabul. Confidence is contagious, and they are determined to spread it wherever they can.

CHAPTER 7

Yekaba Abimbola

When Yekaba was twelve years old, her older sister came running to her with terrifying news: their parents had decided to marry Yekaba to a *twenty-year-old* deacon at their church. She didn't know him—she'd never even seen him—but the deal was worked out between the elders of the church and her father, who was also one of the priests.

At first, Yekaba just didn't believe it. She was only twelve! Although she knew that these kinds of marriages happened all the time in her country, she just didn't think her father would pack her off like that. So she confronted her parents about it, and, to her horror, her father said it was true. There were two daughters left at home, he explained, and he could only afford to send one of them to school. So if her sister went, then Yekaba would have to get married.

Ethiopia, Yekaba's home, is a beautiful country in the Horn of Africa, with mountains and deserts, tropical forests and lush lakes, and some unique species of animals that aren't found anywhere else on the planet. Unfortunately, for girls, it's also a country that has one of the highest rates of early child marriages in the world. Forty percent of Ethiopian girls are married before their eighteenth birthday, many of them before they reach fifteen.

As we found out on Girls Not Brides, 71 percent of child marriages in Ethiopia are arranged by adults. And across the world, a girl under eighteen is married off every two seconds, which adds up to twelve million girls a year. The Ethiopian government, working with the United Nations, has pledged to eliminate child marriage by 2030.

Getting married so young usually ends a girl's education, which means that she has fewer options about what she wants to be when she grows up. It makes it harder for her to earn a living; she is totally dependent on her husband

and his family, and that often means that she starts having children when she is still just a child herself.

Later, you will read about Celia, a girl across the world from Yekaba whose education almost ended early for different reasons.

There are international laws banning child marriage, but there are still plenty of places around the world where the practice thrives and has devastating costs to girls' health, opportunities, and lives. Yekaba's mother hated the plan to marry Yekaba off and objected to it, but her father insisted. He truly felt that this marriage was in their best interest. The husband-to-be came from a wealthy family, and her father was sure that this kind of connection would be an advantage for all of them, including Yekaba's brothers.

Most girls who are pressed into marriages like this don't have the ability to say no. But Yekaba wasn't the kind of girl who was prepared to simply accept her fate. She was determined to put up a fight and try to stop the marriage.

CONFIDENCE BUILDING BLOCK

Risk!

Lucky for her, Yekaba was armed with information about child marriage. She'd learned about it during a two-year program at school run by a humanitarian group that works for kids' rights all over the world, the Girls Advocacy Alliance, part of Plan International. So she used that powerful tool of education and presented her case to her father.

Yekaba asked him if he'd really thought about the health problems she'd face if she got pregnant at twelve years old, especially since she hadn't reached puberty and her body hadn't yet fully developed. She reminded him of her cousin's story. Married at twelve, a mother at fourteen, her cousin was then rejected by her husband, who complained that she didn't do enough housework. Once she was sent back to her parents' house, she lived in limbo—no longer a child, no longer a student, no longer a wife. And her baby was very unhealthy.

At first, Yekaba told us, "It seemed like he was listening to me," thanks to all her evidence. But then: "The man's family came to our house bringing bread. It's a traditional symbol around these parts when a man makes a formal proposal for marriage. And my father accepted the bread, meaning he had accepted the proposal."

Most people in her community were pressuring her to do the "right thing" and go ahead with the marriage. They were baffled at her desire to stay in school, since girls' education is just not considered as important as boys' education. After all, as soon as she got married, she wouldn't need an education to be a good wife and mother. A couple of elders even said to her, "What are you thinking—that you are equal to boys?"

CONFIDENCE QUICKSAND

Stereotyping!

By continuing to protest, Yekaba was taking a big risk. "When I thought of what my family would say when I refused to marry," she explains, "I was so stressed. It was difficult for me even to talk to my father, because adults are to be feared. Children who say no to their parents' plans and interests are considered ill-mannered and unruly. I was also worried about how the community would treat my parents if they broke their promise, not to mention how they would treat me."

She talked to her friends for advice, and they agreed that, no matter what, she had to stop this marriage. They all knew girls in their neighborhoods whose lives had been ruined, and some of her friends had also faced the same thing.

As she'd been taught in her awareness training, there were practical strategies for what to do.

Step 1: Let people know. She thought that if people with more authority than her father in her community (which is known as a *kebele* in Ethiopia) learned about her situation, like leaders at the school, then they might be able to help persuade her father.

So she wrote a note explaining the upcoming marriage and placed it in the box at school dedicated to just these kinds of appeals. (Little did she know, but her good friend Woyzer had also written a cry for help about her, too. You see, girls help each other all over the world.)

Step 2: Create your team. Almost immediately, Yekaba rallied her team of allies. The school principal, representatives and facilitators from the girls' program, her auntie, Ayalnesh, who happens to be the head of the Women and Children's Affairs Office in her *kebele* (and a former child bride herself), and other female relatives all quickly came to her side. So Yekaba wasn't fighting alone.

Step 3: Tell your truth. Right away, her allies listened to what she had to say, heard about what she wanted in her heart. That was incredibly powerful, to have her voice truly heard.

Then one by one, they flocked to see her father, repeating the same evidence that Yekaba had given him and also reminding him that there are some laws in place to protect these girls. Even though those laws are frequently ignored, they do exist. Ayalnesh was blunt with her brother-in-law, telling him she'd take him to court if necessary.

Yekaba's father explained his side of the argument. In his own way, he was trying to protect her future. He was worried that since he was getting older, she would need another man to take care of her.

Yekaba knew he had nothing to worry about there. She let him know that, empowered by her education, she would definitely be able to take care of herself. She didn't need a man to do it.

Finally, after listening to all the lobbying, her dad understood Yekaba's determination and he agreed to cancel the wedding, allowing her to stay in school. He even told Yekaba that he is really excited to see what she can do with her new life.

Today, after fighting for it so hard, Yekaba treasures her education even more. She relishes the time she spends in the school building, diving into higher levels of chemistry and biology, and working with her favorite teachers and all those loyal allies who came to her aid. Even the two-hour-long walk to her school doesn't faze her, since it gives her time with two other girls (whose marriages were also halted) to quiz each other and work out things together that they didn't understand in class.

She's planning to be a doctor because she wants to serve her country and to show what women can accomplish when they are given the chance. The next time a little girl objects to a forced marriage, Yekaba wants to be an example of how to prevail. She's learned that true confidence comes from taking chances, making your own decisions as much as you are able, and pushing through on your own path. What does she want to say to girls around the world in seemingly impossible circumstances?

"It's up to them to become the women of their dreams."

Just Asking

What's your favorite comfort food
that makes everything better?

Injera (Ethiopian flatbread) with sauce

What's the one thing that
you couldn't live without?

Education

If you were an animal, what would you be?

A patient, peaceful cow

What's the one place you've always
wanted to go—your dream destination?

America

What or who always makes you laugh?

Lots of things, but nothing in particular

What do you like to do on a lazy day?

Talk with friends

#FreePeriods

CHAPTER 8

Amika George

For Amika, reading a single article changed her life. One afternoon she was scrolling through the news when something caught her eye. It was a story describing girls who were missing school because they couldn't afford menstrual products (pads and tampons) when they had their periods. She was shocked to learn that "period poverty," as it's called, happens to girls

Not just the menstrual products! Period poverty is also the lack of access to public bathrooms, hand-washing stations, and education.

In Dexa's chapter later on, you'll see this in a village in rural Nepal!

across the world, in every country, including England, where she lives.

Worried about the humiliation of bleeding onto their uniforms or chairs, often too embarrassed to even tell parents or teachers, many girls can be forced to stay home. By some estimates, five hundred million girls around the world can't attend school for about a week every single month. It's hard to even do the math on all that lost time and learning—it would add up to years.

As a teenage girl herself, juggling puberty and parents and school pressure, Amika could relate to both the stress and embarrassment. After all these centuries, menstruation is still treated like a shameful secret instead of something that is natural and actually allows the human race to continue, even though literally half the people on the planet have to deal with it at some point. And girls who don't have the money for the necessary supplies suffer.

This statistic comes from FIGO, the International Federation of Gynecology and Obstetrics.

Amika's mission was to make sure that period empowerment will be seen as a human right and no girl will ever have to miss out on school during her period again. So she started a petition that became a powerful movement all over England, and #freeperiods was born.

Amika's Q&A

How did you feel when you found out about this widespread problem of period poverty?

First I couldn't believe it, then I was shocked it was such an unknown crisis. The idea that girls would have to make a choice between not going to school or

For this book of real stories, we asked Emma Watson, a.k.a. Hermione Granger, a.k.a. Belle, a.k.a. actor and UN Women Goodwill Ambassador and campaigner for girls' empowerment everywhere, to nominate a confident girl. Emma chose Amika George, and here's what Emma told us:

"If you are ever feeling despondent about the possibility of political change or frustrated that the voices of young people aren't heard, then reading about Amika's campaigning will give you hope. Amika brought the issue of period poverty into the public spotlight in a way the UK government could no longer ignore. Her campaigning is joyful as well as fierce and has led to quick and concrete changes to government policy and funding. As a fellow Brit, she's a great inspiration to me and I hope she will motivate many more girls and young women to hold their governments accountable for creating a safe and equal society for all."

using horrific alternatives to sanitary pads and tampons like toilet paper or old socks or newspaper just seemed almost primitive.

I just started to think about what it must be like to have to miss that much school just because of purely economic reasons. When I miss a day of school, I have an insane amount to catch up on, so I can't imagine what it's like to miss a week regularly.

Talking to my friends and family, it turned out no one had heard of period poverty even though it touches so many girls. And when it's in the news, nobody wants to talk about it. It occurred to me that the government wasn't doing anything about it, or even condemning it as an issue to try to change.

I realized, right, there's a taboo about periods in the first place. Nobody wants to talk about them at all. But that silence is hurting girls. And it's isolating them, both socially and academically, which also hurts them.

You know, we think so much has changed in

the last century in women's rights and gender equality, but then again, so much also hasn't.

So, you are a teenager, wanting to make a difference. What was your first step?

I started a petition at Change.org calling for the government to provide supplies for free to the girls who couldn't afford them in schools and colleges in England. I thought it would be a good solution since those girls are already on a list for needing assistance, like free meals, so it shouldn't be too hard. I named it #freeperiods.

CONFIDENCE QUICKSAND

overthinking!

At first I was really worried that I wouldn't even get fifty signatures. Or that nobody would listen. It seemed a little scary that I could send it out there and there could be utter silence.

I was trying hard to get those fifty signatures at first, which felt like a huge task. And then I started a Twitter account for it, and whenever somebody with a considerable number of followers followed me, I asked them to retweet it. I was just being persistent. I was trying to get as much attention as I could. So I was shameless and quite unembarrassed to send the petition to everybody I knew or people I hardly knew and ask them to sign it. It wasn't at all easy to get people sharing and retweeting and reposting but it did work.

I wanted to address both aspects of the period poverty issue: girls having to miss school and the period taboo. Keeping that in public consciousness was important.

Sounds like you harnessed the power of social media. Do you think it helped you get your message out there?

I was a seventeen-year-old girl doing this in my bedroom, but I was able to communicate with thousands and thousands of people just through the internet. It was positive.

And I think that's where activism is headed now. That's why there are so many teenagers who are so politically engaged and getting involved in social issues that they care about. We have this tool that allows us to spread messages and connect with people and organize and mobilize. That power obviously didn't exist in the past.

And it changes our idea of conventional politics.

In the UK, Parliament is increasingly distant for young people, because we don't associate those kinds of politics with our lives. But when you post something on Instagram, or tweet about something that you care about, that's our politics. You're making your voice heard, and you're trying to make change by communicating with other people about issues that matter to you.

I was a little worried that I didn't have any special training or media experience or anything, but it didn't matter. I could still get this message out there.

A lot of adults think if you're on Instagram, you're doing something completely unimportant or you're wasting your time. But actually, I think when teenagers are on their phones, they can be doing amazing and beneficial things for society.

Amika has been outspoken in talking about periods. Usually in public, people practically whisper about them and act very squeamish. Even girls and women can be quite discreet, even secretive.

Was it ever hard for YOU to talk about periods so openly? Were you ever embarrassed?

I was lucky to grow up in an environment where everyone was very feminist and empowered. I went to a girls' school. My parents, and even my younger brother, were open with me, talking about blood, leaking, staining and all the rest. It seemed normal. So I was comfortable talking about it publicly from the beginning.

But a couple of months into it, I realized that most people don't have the same attitude. Some of my friends told me that they only told their moms six months after starting their periods because of the taboo. And they would never even consider telling their brothers or dads.

This embarrassment was definitely a hindrance in the campaign. I was taken less seriously by politicians, just because it was about periods. Our Parliament is made up of 70 percent men. One of them even refused to say the word *tampon*.

stereotyping!

But it feels like there's a huge revolution in the way that people are treating periods now. Every single time I go on Instagram, I discover someone talking about it very openly.

After the petition, things took off quickly. Amika has written articles, given talks, partnered with groups like the Pink Protest, and organized a powerful peaceful protest that attracted celebrities, influencers, and supporters from all over. And she has gotten through to policy makers in the British government.

Where do things stand now with your campaign?

In the middle of March this year, I was sitting in the library doing an essay for school. I got a notification on my phone saying that the chancellor of the UK has pledged to provide free products in all schools and colleges in the UK starting in 2020. Of course, that's great, but I also think it's bigger than this—it's becoming this bigger movement.

It would be a dream if this next generation of children grew up treating periods as a perfectly normal part of conversations, like what they had for dinner, free of any stigma.

Just Asking

What's your favorite comfort food
that makes everything better?

Tea

What's the one thing that you
couldn't live without?

My friends and family

If you were an animal, what would you be?

An elephant

What's the one place you've always wanted
to go—your dream destination?

China

What or who always makes you laugh?

My brother

What do you like to do on a lazy day?

Watch TV with my friends. Eat quite a lot.

CHAPTER 9

Sam Gordon

S am has always loved sports. Nothing beats running, sweating, kicking, pushing, and, above all, *competing*. Definitely competing. Sam is a tough, speedy, determined outside back on her soccer team. She idolizes Alex Morgan and Abby Wambach, and is working toward state and even national championships this year. Her big dream is to play professional soccer in the future.

But the sport that Sam loves even more than soccer is a sport that's rarely played by girls: American football. She's a tough, speedy, and determined quarterback and linebacker. Still, Sam has had to work hard and fight hard to convince people that girls can play football as well as boys. (Obviously, they can!) Starting when she was in grade school, Sam has had to prove to her teammates, their parents, and the coaches that she can play the game.

There was one person she didn't have to convince, one person who completely believed in and agreed with her: her dad.

About five years ago, after clawing her way onto several teams and, as she says, knocking boys on their butts, Sam and her father decided to found a girls' tackle football league. They wanted to make sure that other girls got the opportunity to participate in this sport they love and to create a community that supports them, instead of judging or limiting them.

Since she's also so passionate about soccer and plays it intensely, too, we asked Sam about what makes *football* special and so important to her.

"Football is different than other sports. It takes fighting. Every single play is like a new opportunity to score a touchdown, a new opportunity for you to make a difference. And that makes it an intense team sport. It builds the team, as everybody has to support each other and do everything together. It's such a great energy and girls come together like best friends. But maybe the best part is that anybody can play it.

"There's so many different positions in football, there's room for every single body type, there's something for everybody. In soccer you have to be able to run like crazy up and down the field, or in basketball on the court. But with football, it's not just one kind of skill. We can put one girl on the line to get through and sack the quarterback, or another girl can make big blocks and be crucial to the team with a different kind of skill. It can change girls' lives to be MVP or an all-star. Football makes girls confident, gives us leadership skills, and builds us into a family."

Everyone in Sam's own family is super into football, going to local games and watching their favorite teams on TV. She's been throwing the ball around at recess with other kids or after dinner with neighbors and her dad, brothers, and little sister for as long as she can remember. When Sam was about nine, her older brother started to play seriously on a team of other twelve-year-olds. She'd go to the practices to watch, and she got totally hooked. At the end of the practices, the boys would run wind sprints, and so she decided to run them, too. She beat most of the players the first time, and then it became a thing: she ran with the team at every practice and beat them.

After one of these practices, the coach suggested that she try out for the next season, which planted the idea in her head. For the next few months, she trained as hard as she could to improve her speed and agility, with drills, drills, and more drills. When tryouts came, it all paid off when she competed against the boys and placed first in many of the drills, including sacking. She says some boys would chant "Beat the girl, beat the girl," and even some parents would yell "Don't get beat by a girl!" None of it fazed her.

That is, until she was placed on one of the lower-level teams and boys that she beat were picked ahead of her. This was an eye-opening moment.

"I asked my dad why I didn't get onto one of the higher-level teams, even though I proved that

I should be. And he explained that it was just because I was a girl and they weren't used to me going out and playing football. I was raised to do whatever I wanted, and I never thought that I might be held back because of being a girl. Instead of quitting or getting ridiculously upset (of course I was upset), I just decided that I was going to prove those coaches wrong.

CONFIDENCE BUILDING BLOCK

Rebounding!

"And that's exactly what I did that season. The coach of my team was super supportive of me, my teammates were super supportive. I got to run the ball a lot that season and ended up scoring like thirty-five touchdowns, two thousand rushing yards, sixty-eight tackles—those types of statistics. My dad ended up putting up a highlight video of that first season and it kind of went viral."

It most definitely went viral! Over the next couple years, Sam kept playing football with the boys, and people everywhere were paying attention to this lone girl trying to make a place for other girls in the sport. Her nickname became Sweet Feet, since she jumped all over the place. She felt like she had a bit of a target on her back, but every game gave her the chance to change minds.

"I'd walk up to the field and everybody would be like, 'Oh, cute little girl.' Then we'd play and by the second half they're all like, 'Oh my gosh, GET that girl.' It's cool when they actually start believing that girls are more than just 'cute.'"

She wound up on TV, visiting schools all over the country, and even on a Wheaties box! At some point, Sam started to realize that at five feet tall, she couldn't play against boys who were growing to be double or triple her size. But her favorite things were still playing the game and talking about girls playing the game.

At eleven, Sam was speaking to a middle school assembly. She looked around the room and had a game-changing idea.

"I asked the question: How many girls here would want to play tackle football? And it seemed like almost every hand in the room went up, and that was a light-bulb moment for me. If there are this many here, imagine how many there are in the state of Utah or the whole country. Then it all kind of clicked: I wanted to see more girls out there playing. I'd had friends come up to me and say that they wanted to play, but that their parents weren't comfortable with them up against the boys, they didn't want them to get hurt. But then it came together in my mind: girls playing against other girls."

She and her dad, who's a lawyer, consulted with some other friends and formed the **Utah Girls Tackle Football League** in their Salt Lake City suburb just a few weeks later. The first season was a bit ragged, since hardly any of the girls had ever played the sport. But it grew. Starting with fifty girls, the league expanded to five hundred girls in four years, with teams at the elementary, middle, and high school level. Girls' football takes an incredible combination of speed,

According to the Women's Football Alliance, there are three girls' leagues in the country: Utah Girls Tackle Football, Georgia Girls Tackle Football, and Indiana Girls Tackle Football League.

strength, agility, ball handling, and strategy. Sam herself has never gone back to playing against the boys. At sixteen, she is all about *girls'* tackle football.

And their games are packed now, with parents lined up along the sides, fans hollering, concessions handing out hot dogs, and, as Sam says, "girls playing 100 percent. Like a legit high school football experience."

It's still disheartening, though, that this girls' football league has to buy its own gear, rent spaces, and coordinate memberships and games, instead of being able to let the girls play football at their local high schools, like the boys do. According to a bill passed over forty years ago to guarantee equal treatment for girls, called Title IX, girls' teams should have the same funding and support as the boys', except they don't. Very few schools have girls' football teams.

So Sam and her father have sued high schools and their districts to try to create opportunities for girls to play football as an officially sanctioned team sport. They've made some progress, but there's still a way to go. Sam's disappointed that they are getting pushback. She says, "I want to see it grow across the nation and become something strong in high schools, in colleges, even a professional league." She also gets that it will take time, and that she may well be too old to play in it.

That makes her a little sad, but she knows from playing both football and soccer that you can't win every play or every game. Still, you've got to keep trying, refocus, and move on. Sam works hard to stop overthinking, or "spazzing out," as she calls it. One of her coaches taught her a trick when she needs to reset her brain, a physical cue to switch gears. With one arm at her side, she gives her hand a little shake—that shake has become a signal to put everything else aside and look to the next play.

There are lots of strategies to help change the channel in your brain when negative thinking kicks in. Listen to music, take a walk, hit the Pause button, and take a hot minute to just breathe deeply—or, like Sam, give your hand a little shake!

She told us, "The confidence from sports definitely translates into everything else around me, like body confidence.

A lot of girls struggle with that, but I've never felt down about myself.

"In sports, it's not about how you look, it's really just like what you can do and how your body is actually an advantage. You don't need to look the perfect way, you just know that you can go out there and do it."

Just Asking

What's your favorite comfort food
that makes everything better?

Raspberries

What's the one thing that you
couldn't live without?

My friends (or my phone)

If you were an animal, what would you be?

A cheetah

What's the one place you've always wanted
to go—your dream destination?

Paris

What or who always makes you laugh?

My older brother

What do you like to do on a lazy day?

Binge-watch TV

CHAPTER 10

Taylor Fuentes

Taylor has always thrown herself, passionately, with tremendous spirit and a huge smile, into everything she does. In grade school in sunny California, Taylor would tear it up at recess with high energy, playing mostly with boys, getting dirty and being silly, without worrying about what other people thought.

The twelve-year-old is obsessed with purple, so she often wears it head to toe and puts dazzling stripes of it in her hair. Taylor also loves bold patterns and wild socks, pulling on mismatched pairs to add to the fun. And she paints uplifting and cheery messages on rocks and leaves them all over town.

These days, though, some of Taylor's infectious energy is consumed by a less lighthearted subject—bullying. Unfortunately, it's something she knows way too much about. For two terrifying years, she suffered at the hands of some vicious bullies at her school. Now she's turning her passion into talking to girls, usually in Girl Scout troops, about recognizing bullying, building resilience, getting help, and fighting back.

For Taylor, the nightmare of her own bullying started early.

Up until third grade, Taylor had just gone about doing all the cool stuff she liked to do. She loved school and did really well. She may not have had a ton of friends, but she also didn't really think about it. Part of her knew that she was a bit of an outsider to most of the girls, with the purple and the socks and all of that, but most of the time, she just did her own unique things.

Apparently, a lot of the girls at her school really didn't like Taylor's unique things. First they attacked her for hanging out with boys. Taylor has three brothers and likes to play football and dodgeball and zombies. Most of the time, she was the only girl on the playground who joined those kinds of games.

Other girls accused her of trying to be cooler than

they were or being a traitor to girls. They criticized what she liked to do; then they started criticizing everything else about her—her purple passion, the streaks in her hair, the way she talked, or the color of her skin (she's of Mexican descent). Of course, it's impossible to really say what triggers bullies; it never makes sense and it's never OK. But to Taylor, it seemed like everything that made her *her* was everything that set these bullies off.

Once the bullying started, it was relentless.

It came at Taylor from all angles, from not letting her sit down at lunch, to name-calling, to hostile comments on social media, to actual hitting and shoving. She was pushed into a fence outside and constantly bumped, roughly, while standing in lines. The few friends she'd had just kind of faded away.

One time, some girls grabbed her backpack when she was working in the library, dumped it out, and hid all her stuff in far-flung places around the school. Another time, in fourth grade, she was in a bathroom stall and a couple of bullies held the door shut so that she was trapped. When the bell rang and a teacher checked the bathroom, they ran away.

For a while, Taylor kept this to herself, refusing to tell anyone. She was reluctant to be labeled a snitch and didn't really want to get the mean girls in trouble. Plus, Taylor was also afraid that telling people would just make it worse. Much worse. She'd always been really outgoing and happy-go-lucky, but she pulled inward, becoming very quiet and withdrawn.

She toyed with the idea of trying to act more like the bullies to make them stop. But even at her most miserable, she felt that she had to be true to herself. She couldn't cave in. And when they attacked her skin color, she felt such pride in her heritage that she only wanted to dig in even more. No way would she change anything, big or small.

CONFIDENCE BUILDING BLOCK

Authenticity!

She grew to dread school every day, wondering what they'd come up with next. Taylor's really close to her family, but somehow she was too sad and scared to share what was happening with them. She almost didn't want to bring it into her house, to have it infect her private spaces. As she says, "At home, I could get away. I'd go to my room, do my homework, and stay in there all night. I didn't even want to socialize with my family." She would cry for hours, in secret. Sometimes, she'd fake being sick for days in a row, just to hide out, safe and sound, at home.

When her mom noticed the changes in Taylor and these frequent sick days, Taylor finally confided in her.

Her mom immediately notified the school, thinking that would be the end of it. As it turns out, the school was sympathetic but couldn't do much without solid proof or adult witnesses, which is hard to find in ugly hissed comments, mean glares, and secretive shoving.

It was just Taylor's word against her tormentors.

Still, she refused to either sink to their level and get mean, or try to make them like her. Over and over again, Taylor would remind herself of her role models, using them to help her through rough days.

"So, one is fictional and one is real. Hermione Granger was teased for being too shy, too quiet, too smart, and not like everyone else. But she ended up being a hero in the end. And Meghan Markle (the Duchess of Sussex in England) had to face critics, stereotypes, and, in a way, she was bullied, too. She believes that every girl has a voice that should be heard. Every day, I live by her words: 'Confidence is not: they will like me. Confidence is: I'll be fine if they don't.' With that attitude, how could she not be my role model?"

But role models aren't exactly the same as real-life friends and allies.

Then something happened in the middle of fifth grade that got everyone's attention. In PE class, a group of girls circled around her, taunting her. Instead of keeping silent, she used her voice, talking back to them. Suddenly, one of them lunged forward and bit her, really hard, on her back.

Horrible as it was, it was such dramatic evidence of the bullying that it wound up rallying her teachers, the principal, and even the superintendent to stop this harassment.

By this point, Taylor had also found another incredible source of strength and support. She'd joined a California Girl Scout troop with girls from totally different schools. Meeting at the troop leader's house, learning new skills, getting out of her own head, hanging out with a new group of supportive girls—all of this helped Taylor get some distance and perspective. She treasured every minute with her Girl Scout troop, where they practiced archery, created crafts, planted trees, and worked on a sustainable project for her Silver Award. The Girl Scouts really encourage community and the power of sisterhood—and sharing problems is a huge part of that.

Taylor was able to open up to them. "My Girl Scout troop accepted me for how unique and different I am," she says. "All the things that my bullies called my flaws, my Girl Scout sisters loved and accepted as my best qualities.

She's in good company—there are lots of powerful Girl Scouts! Meghan Markle, Taylor Swift, Mariah Carey, Abigail Breslin, Gwyneth Paltrow, Dakota Fanning, Venus and Serena Williams, plus Hillary Clinton, Madeleine Albright, and Condoleezza Rice are just a few. That's not all—72 percent of women senators and 58 percent of congresswomen were Girl Scouts, according to girlscouts.org.

"When people tell you that you're not worthy, it's easy to believe them. But when people open their arms, you learn to believe in yourself."

When sixth grade started in the fall, things were looking up. Way up. Taylor still had classes with her former bullies, but bolstered by her Girl Scout sisters and a new mantra that she repeats over and over— *"don't believe me, just watch,"* from a Bruno Mars song—she had a lot more confidence in facing them. There were still a few girls snickering behind her back, but she refuses to pay any attention. She's got a posse of new friends. Now Taylor knows that she can talk to her teachers, meet new kids, and make new, true friends who support her.

CONFIDENCE
BUILDING
BLOCK

Rebounding
and Resilience!

Lots of people would barely get through something like this, but Taylor has not only survived it, she's been willing to share and be honest about something that both embarrassed and horrified her. Taylor gives talks to younger Girl Scouts and other community groups, to try to empower kids so that bullying doesn't happen to anyone else. She's even spoken at a statewide Girl Scout conference in Sacramento and been profiled in an article on the Girl Scout website. She's fiercely determined to make sure that other kids don't feel as alone as she did.

Remarkably, Taylor has no interest in holding grudges. "I just want everyone to know that they shouldn't be afraid to be themselves," she explained. "And I'm hoping to spread positivity. Everyone should be living in a world where bullying doesn't exist and acceptance does. I want to spread confidence everywhere."

Given her experience, she's realized that one of the most important things that kids can remember about bullying is that when you "see something, say something."

Even if you're not the target of bullies, you can call them out when you see it happening. Stop it in its tracks. Bystanders have a lot of power in bullying situations, so Taylor wants to take the focus off bullies and put it back on ways to help.

Getting through her brutal experience and sharing it with others actually gave her the courage and the confidence to take another risk. Although it was terrifying to put herself out there and she didn't know a single soul doing it, she joined a marching-band drum and bugle corps called the Blue Devils. Taylor is part of the color guard, where she twirls silk flags or nonworking rifles and sabers in elaborate choreography with all kinds of drums and horns.

It's the perfect place for her, waving bright explosions of color in time to music, nestled into an ever-moving sea of people, totally being herself. As she says, "confidence is a superpower," and she's determined to spread her own, hard-won as it is.

Just Asking

What's your favorite comfort food
that makes everything better?

Any type of salad, like fruit salads or green salads

What's the one thing that you
couldn't live without?

My family

If you were an animal, what would you be?

A cat

What's the one place you've always wanted
to go—your dream destination?

Hawaii

What or who always makes you laugh?

My friends

What do you like to do on a lazy day?

Stay home and draw or paint

CHAPTER 11

Genesis Butler

As soon as she could talk, Genesis was full of questions. Like lots of little kids, she would point to just about everything and ask those essential "whys." And, also like lots of little kids, Genesis felt a deep connection to animals. Not only did she revel in their cuteness, she had an intense sensitivity and connection to every animal she ever saw. At an incredibly early age, Genesis was so inspired by her love for animals, she started to wonder about how she wanted to treat them and what she could do to make the planet a kinder, safer, and healthier place for all the creatures who live here.

When she was just about to turn four, Genesis was savoring her favorite dinner: chicken nuggets. She adored them and could eat them all day, every day. That night, she held up one of the tasty morsels and turned to her mom, asking, "Where do chicken nuggets come from?"

First her mom said, "From the grocery store, of course." Genesis chewed on another nugget, and then asked, "No, really, where do they actually come from?" Her mom explained that they came from a chicken that was killed to make the meat. Other meat is the same, her mother told her; it comes from pigs or cows or lambs that are raised to wind up as food. For many people, this is an accepted part of the natural cycle of life, happening in nature every day. Humans have been eating animals since the beginning of time.

But for Genesis, this was horrifying news.

She could picture chickens strutting around, clucking and squawking. She could picture chubby piglets and fluffy lambs and all sorts of other creatures. She remembers feeling that "a chicken is like a sibling. I wouldn't want to eat one of my siblings, like my little sister or my brother, so how could I eat an animal? They're practically the same thing."

But she didn't just think those things and keep them inside her head. For her, it seemed like the best way she could at least try to protect animals was to stop eating them. She set down her fork and never ate another bite of meat again. That very night, she and her mom, impressed by Genesis's sense of purpose, became determined vegetarians.

A couple of years later, she had a similar eye-opening revelation. She was sitting with her mom, who was breastfeeding her baby sister. Genesis wondered aloud about where we get the milk we drink—where does it come from? Her mom explained that it usually comes from the mama cows, who are producing it for their babies, but some of it gets bottled and sent to people instead.

Genesis was shocked. To her, it made no sense. What if someone took her mother's milk away from her baby sister? She didn't think that would be fair, so she didn't think human beings should do that to cows, either. As she likes to say:

"We share this planet with animals, so we're all in it together."

So once again, she made a vow, this time to not consume any dairy or anything else that comes from animals: no eggs, no milk, no cheese, no ice cream, no yogurt, no honey. She was so passionate and persuasive that, this time, her *whole* family decided to support her by joining in. Her parents and her siblings, along with Genesis, all became vegan after that. It was their way to try to make a difference.

Vegans do not eat or wear anything that comes from animals (milk, eggs, meat, leather, or fur). They also don't believe in testing on animals, or in zoos, circuses, or anything that uses animals as entertainment, like horse or dog racing, according to vegansociety.com.

It wasn't easy—there were definitely things she missed. Genesis longed for hot, cheesy pizza or rich, delicious cake with icing, especially since it seemed like those foods were tempting her everywhere she turned, at birthday parties and family potlucks. She asked her mom if they could *"veganize"* her favorite foods so she wouldn't have to totally give them up.

By looking harder at the grocery store, diving deep into the colorful fresh fruits and vegetables, and also discovering all the amazing vegan options like vegan cheese and even vegan nuggets, she and her family have found an abundance of delicious food that doesn't come from animals. Genesis says she felt in her heart that this was not only the right thing for her to do for her beloved animals, but the right thing to do for a planet in trouble.

Ariana Grande, Miley Cyrus, Beyoncé, Zac Efron, Ellie Goulding, and Venus Williams are just some of the many famous folks who eat a plant-based diet!

By the time Genesis was about seven, her questioning led her and her parents to do more research on what's called ethical veganism and the ways that animals are often treated, especially on big factory farms, when they are exclusively raised to be meat. With her parents' help, she started going to animal rights protests and events, learning more about the relationship between raising animals for food and climate change. She found out that animal agriculture (growing animals in order to eat them) requires literally tons of grain, in addition to enormous quantities of water, to produce a small portion of meat.

Here's an example that Genesis likes to use from her

research: the same amount of water that she uses for two months of five-minute showers would only produce one hamburger. One burger for one person—gallons and gallons of water. So if you add that up for the six billion people across the world who eat meat, then all those resources could really make a difference toward solving water shortages, food scarcity, and even climate change (when animals poop, they emit methane and other gases that contribute to global warming).

As we learned from the US Geological Survey Water Science School, it takes 460 gallons of water for about a quarter pound of ground beef.

"It's the most important time to go vegan," Genesis told us, "because climate change is happening so quickly. The planet is being destroyed, so we have to do something about it. Veganism is one of the main things that we can do to stop climate change. It will really work."

Genesis decided that she wanted to go beyond just what she could do on her own and join forces with other people in this fight—to make her voice more heard. The more of these rallies and meetings that she attended, the more she felt that she could help.

Even though she was so young—usually the youngest by far everywhere she went—she got the hang of activism pretty quickly. She figured out that handing out leaflets can really spread the message, and that, even as a kid, there are plenty of ways to contribute. For one thing, starting a chant really gets people pumped. At one of her first protests, she hopped up to the mic and shouted her favorite declaration about how connected we all are: "one struggle, one fight, human freedom, animal rights."

Talking in front of crowds at rallies did make her super nervous at first. But Genesis was able to remind herself that it's not about her. She's speaking for creatures who have no voice.

That's a really good trick for taking risks and building up confidence—when something feels intimidating, think about doing it for someone, or something, else.  Something you care about, something you believe in. For Genesis, when she talks about animals, her anxiety slips away.

CONFIDENCE BUILDING BLOCK

ME to WE!

After a while, Genesis started to look for even more tangible ways to protect animals and the planet. One of her first projects was called Meatless Monday. An animal-rights activist group called Farm Sanctuary asked her to join its campaign to get cities, schools, and communities to take a break from meat on Mondays by helping make her hometown of Long Beach, California, next on the list. She knew she couldn't expect everyone to make the leap to becoming vegan all at once. But starting with baby steps, convincing them to try a different option once a week, seemed possible.

Farm Sanctuary is an organization devoted to changing the way farm animals are treated. They run farms in California and New York for chickens, sheep, pigs, cows, turkeys, and goats rescued from abusive situations.

She talked about it first at school and then to an even bigger audience at the Long Beach City Council. The resolution passed for California's fifth-largest city, promoting a break from meat one day a week. It's not a law, so people don't have to obey it, but Genesis thinks it's a good step.

Since Genesis's big goal is to "get the whole entire

world to go vegan," she knows she has a long way to go. And it won't be a straight line, an easy path. She has to live with the fact that failure happens. She can try hard and put in tons of time, travel, and effort, but it doesn't always work.

Sometimes it does seem like things are moving slowly. One of Genesis's biggest challenges is getting frustrated. And like most people, she doesn't like dealing with failure. Recently, she was working with some folks

Perfectionism!

at an organization called the Million Dollar Vegan campaign to convince the pope to go vegan for the forty days of Lent, in exchange for a million-dollar donation to charity. Unfortunately, the plan didn't work. The pope didn't take their challenge, and he kept eating whatever it is that popes eat. She was disappointed— pretty bummed out.

And sometimes people at school or online have been rude to her, picking on her, questioning whether any of this will matter. This can be really discouraging, too. Rallies can sometimes be rough if there are lots of counterprotesters there, shouting at her.

When things like that happen, Genesis can get really

down. But gradually, she's learned not to dwell on it.

CONFIDENCE BUILDING BLOCK

Rebounding!

Genesis has a cool confidence strategy. She focuses on something that brings her comfort. For her, it's actually her own name, which means *beginning*. When she feels stress start to build, she tries to focus on a new start—on what's next—and that gets her back to what's really important.

"This is a very good time for people to become activists since there are lots of fellow activists to work with and get strength from. We do need more kid activists, because kids really care. Right now we have to fight for our planet. I'm twelve, and I know how fast that time has gone by. We really have to hurry before time is up."

Just Asking

What's your favorite comfort food that makes everything better?

Vegan mac and cheese

What's the one thing that you couldn't live without?

My friends and my family

If you were an animal, what would you be?

A wolf. Wolves can be shy sometimes, but if they really need to do something, they'll use their voice.

What's the one place you've always wanted to go—your dream destination?

Paris

What or who always makes you laugh?

My friends' funny jokes

What do you like to do on a lazy day?

Lie around and watch Netflix

CHAPTER 12

Greta Thunberg

A girl and a sign. That's how it began. In Stockholm, fifteen-year-old Greta Thunberg balanced a hand-painted piece of wood on her bike and rode to the parliament building. Sitting alone on the sidewalk, she challenged her government to DO something about climate change. She called it a climate strike, because she did this instead of going to school as usual. Greta has been completely consumed by climate change since she was little. "Some people can just let things go," she has said, when talking about what got her started. "But I can't, especially if there's something that worries me or makes me sad." After a long, dark period of depression, Greta figured out that she has autism, specifically Asperger's syndrome, which also gives her a single-minded focus that can be overwhelming, or empowering. Her passion, or obsession, for the environment actually helped her recover from her depression. She was able to motivate herself by taking action.

You read about Ciara-Beth earlier in the book, another girl using her autism as a strength!

First, she talked her parents into joining her as a vegan to lower the family's carbon footprint. Then she convinced her mom, who flew all the time, to give up air travel because of the planes' toxic emissions into the atmosphere. Being able to make these changes in her family gave her hope and made her realize that she could turn her "disability" into an incredible asset. Today, of course, she is no longer sitting alone on a sidewalk. She's talked to world leaders, been on the cover of *Time* magazine, been nominated for a Nobel Peace Prize, and rallied millions of kids around the world into a global community trying to protect our planet and their future.

CHAPTER 13

Mena & Zena Nasiri

Mena and Zena had each been given a pretty standard fourth-grade homework assignment at their Minnesota grade school: write about someone you look up to and admire. The sisters, who are a year apart, each charged to her local public library when she got the assignment, first one, then the other a year later. They were excited to read the adventures of any of the amazing women their mom had told them stories about, only to find . . . nothing. Not one thing. Not one book on the important historical Muslim women they'd heard about growing up. Or any other Muslim women.

And that's when they first started to notice, to

really notice, that when they looked around the shelves, Muslim kids, Muslim characters, even common Muslim names pretty much didn't exist. As bookworms, Mena and Zena had been eagerly devouring all sorts of stories throughout their lives without ever noticing they were not seeing themselves in those pages. There weren't kids like them in any of the picture books when they were little, chapter books or novels when they got older, or biographies when it came time to write reports.

"Reading was prioritized in our house," Zena, who is a year older than her sister, told us. "Our parents are immigrants from Iraq and they want us to have the best education and the best lives possible. So reading was always emphasized and we both love books and we grew up in the library. Books gave us more understanding and we knew how much they meant.

"So when we realized that as Muslim girls, we weren't represented, we knew it mattered."

When that exact same thing happened to her the

next year, Mena remembers, "that's the first time it sunk in that there was such a lack of representation and diversity at the library." It wasn't until later, in eighth and ninth grade, that they finally read a book with a Muslim main character: *The Lines We Cross* by Randa Abdel-Fattah. Everything changed. It replaced that feeling of not belonging from when they were in grade school with an indescribable feeling of connecting. And suddenly, they were motivated to act.

For a start, they wanted their school library to include plenty of stories about kids like them. Their parents helped them come up with a plan. To put the plan in action, Mena says the first step was to go to their PTA. "We asked them to give us $150 to buy books from a list that we made so we could put these books in the individual school media centers."

You will read more about the importance of seeing people like you in the world—representation—in Jamie's story later in the book.

Sounds easier than it was. Were they nervous about getting up at an official meeting, pitching their idea to a group of adults, and asking for money? Um, YES!

"The presentation to the PTA was kind of a big thing," Zena explains. "We had to be taken out of school for it. It was our first one, and it was definitely scary. We're both shy and it was hard."

Luckily, the girls could rely on each other to push through the challenging part and manage that fear. For Zena, "Being together is helpful. I knew that if I messed up, Mena would cover for me and have my back and the other way around. It seemed a lot scarier at first, but the PTA was nice and supportive the entire time."

Mena told us that, for her, focusing on *why* they were there helped. "It was something that we wanted to do. It was so important to us and we knew that we had to get over our fear eventually. We just knew that we had to do it."

Following through paid off. Right away, they got two hundred books into their school libraries, and that victory gave them a taste to do even more! They wanted more books, more libraries, more representation! They raised money for books from neighbors and friends, and then a good friend of their mom's suggested starting a nonprofit organization.

Nonprofits are businesses that don't try to make money, but instead do good things with the money they earn or that people donate. With the help of others, nonprofits can achieve some incredibly cool stuff. The girls were sure that having a nonprofit would give them more opportunities and credibility, too. "It seems more official and better than two girls going around just asking people for money," Mena explains, "especially considering our age."

They named their nonprofit **Girls of the Crescent**, for the crescent moon that symbolizes Islam. Then they launched their book campaign with a cool hashtag, #muslimgirlsread2. The business part was more than a little overwhelming, with all the legal forms and paperwork and more legal forms and more paperwork, but their mom's friend guided them through the whole thing. That helped a lot.

Other things took a lot of effort, too. Researching, buying, and cataloging new books, figuring out where to donate them, and writing for newspapers and websites, plus doing interviews for TV or books (like this one!). It's a ton of pressure. Not to mention, the better Girls of the Crescent does, the more people are interested in the message, adding more work on top of homework on top

CONFIDENCE QUICKSAND

People-pleasing!

of more work on top of . . . You get the point! Zena also told us that being in the spotlight as a Muslim American can be frightening at times, that it felt risky because "it puts our identities out there and people might not agree with what we are doing."

But she and her sister have learned to get through the doubts, to pay little attention to negative comments or discouraging people. They are working on how to better deal with both the big challenges and everyday failures. Zena clearly remembers one of those: "I recently got a bad grade on a math test. I panicked and cried. But then I thought, it's not the end of the world and I can take other tests. Next time, I will work harder."

Mena and Zena admit they are often too hard on themselves—too perfectionistic—which might hurt their confidence. But they say there's extra pressure on them to maintain that perfect image.

CONFIDENCE QUICKSAND

Stereotyping!

Zena explains, "As Muslim girls, we are not always held to a standard that we think we should be. We are underestimated a lot, and we want to prove ourselves. Girls of the Crescent is helping with that. Books can open people's eyes to different perspectives and can hopefully turn the narrative away from the 'oppressed Muslim girl' to a Muslim girl who can fight for herself and do amazing things without the influence of society's negative stereotypes."

Now, through Girls of the Crescent, they have collected hundreds of books for over twenty-one schools in their Minnesota district and donated more to public libraries and other schools as far away as Texas and Pakistan. They are constantly adding to their growing list of book titles to share with collections around the world, to make sure library shelves are full of strong Muslim characters. To celebrate the first anniversary of Girls of the Crescent, the *Today* show came to their house and did a piece about them. "It was probably

Mena & Zena's original fourth-grade sheroes:

Mena: "Fatima al-Fihri, who built the world's first university."

Zena: "Sabiha Gökçen, the first woman fighter pilot in the world, who was Turkish."

the biggest moment so far and shows how much we've grown in just a year!" Mena says.

So now, when fourth graders (or any graders!) troop into libraries in Rochester, Minnesota, or any of the other places where Mena and Zena have expanded the collections, they can find out all about Sabiha and Fatima and tons of other amazing Muslim people, both real and fictional!

"My friend actually recently read one of my favorite books on our list about a female Muslim," Mena remembers, "and after she read it, she came up to me and said it was eye-opening. It kind of gave her a new perspective. She couldn't stop talking about it for weeks, which shows that these books can be influential."

Mena & Zena's recommendations:

☆ *THE LINES WE CROSS* by Randa Abdel-Fattah

☆ *UNDER THE PERSIMMON TREE* by Suzanne Fisher Staples

☆ *GOLDEN DOMES AND SILVER LANTERNS* by Hena Khan

☆ *THE LIBRARIAN OF BASRA* by Jeanette Winter

☆ *AYESHA DEAN: THE ISTANBUL INTRIGUE* by Melati Lum

☆ *MS. MARVEL* by G. Willow Wilson and Sana Amanat

Just Asking

What's your favorite comfort food that makes everything better?

Zena: Chocolate   **Mena:** Ice cream

What's the one thing that you couldn't live without?

Zena: My journal   **Mena:** My art supplies

If you were an animal, what would you be?

Zena: A duck   **Mena:** A penguin

What's the one place you've always wanted to go—your dream destination?

Zena: Hawaii   **Mena:** Switzerland

What or who always makes you laugh?

Zena: Mena   **Mena:** Zena

What do you like to do on a lazy day?

Zena: Read   **Mena:** Read, too

CHAPTER 14

Adelle Pritchard

Crepes. Paper-thin pancakes that wrap themselves around any kind of delectable tasty treat you can imagine. Or simply beg to be drizzled with lemon, honey, or cinnamon. Sweet, savory, spicy, creamy—you name it, a crepe of any kind is incredible. Adelle's been obsessed with crepes since she was little.

She has always been super into cooking and baking, loving the way she can express herself through different recipes and combinations. It makes her feel self-reliant and capable, which then encourages her to try more dishes and be even more creative. But when Adelle started making crepes—she knew she'd found her calling.

A crepe as a calling? It can happen! For Adelle, crepes are much more than flour, milk, and eggs. They are her creative passion, and she decided to translate them into a business.

Growing up in the river town of Chattanooga, Tennessee, Adelle was introduced to crepes by her British father. As she says, "There's this thing called Pancake Day in England. It's the same as Mardi Gras, but all about crepes, which is what they mean by pancakes there. For Pancake Day/Mardi Gras at our house, we would make hundreds of crepes with tons of cool fillings and have lots of people over. So I always associated crepes with parties and fun.

"When we'd visit family in England every year, we'd usually go to France as well. I loved all the little street carts with crepes. I've always wanted something like that in Chattanooga, but there wasn't anything. When I was in sixth grade, we traveled to France again, and I realized that if no one was going to do it in my hometown, then I could. There was such a gap in the market. And I wanted to take advantage of that."

Adelle knew starting a business was tricky, even overwhelming. It was definitely a huge risk. She explains, "I was unsure about how to do it. And I hadn't heard of other kids my age doing anything like this. I was worried that it wouldn't work out and that I wouldn't have the time to focus well on either school or the business. What if it fell apart? What if all the effort was for nothing? It was just something so out of my comfort zone. That was the scariest part of it."

CONFIDENCE
BUILDING
BLOCK

Risk!

The more Adelle thought about it, though, the more she was sure that an adorable creperie could definitely succeed. That's when she turned to her parents. They'd both started their own businesses, so they were very encouraging.

It took all three of them about a year to put all the pieces together. And it was a huge learning curve. They had to figure out the equipment, the employees, the logo, the finances, and the location. She and her parents consulted anyone they knew, getting recommendations, setting up meetings with folks in the restaurant business, taking advice from lots of people, until they had gathered as much information as possible. Even though her parents helped her out, Adelle made all the final decisions.

It was like doing a massive research project for school. At first it seemed almost impossible, but they broke the whole concept into small tasks, and bit by bit they got the knowledge they needed. Along the way, Adelle learned something surprising: she deeply cared about all these details, from natural ingredients and hormone-free meat to the way the restaurant would look.

It was a frustrating year, with things moving along at a fast pace and then slowing down to a crawl so it sometimes felt they were making no progress at all. It took loads of patience.

Adelle wanted to start small—she was understandably reluctant to make a big investment and risk losing her savings and her parents' money. She kept trying to have every single aspect planned to the last tiny detail, so that they wouldn't go into debt. But, right before the start of seventh grade, it finally all came together and **Adelle's Ice Cream Creperie** was ready to launch. Adelle was just twelve years old and about to open a restaurant!

As they got close to opening, Adelle planned the

menu. She'd made thousands of crepes at all these family parties over the years and tested the recipes and flavors out on her guests, so this was the part that she knew best. "I wanted the focus to be on crepes and ice cream, because those were the typical elements of the creperies I had seen in France," she explains. "So I came up with a set of five sweet ones and five savory ones."

After all the planning, Adelle still was scared, even though her mom became her business partner. She was worried about letting down all the people who believed in her and terrified of taking the giant leap outside her comfort zone. Still, she just took it one step at a time, focusing on the next piece of her careful plan.

CONFIDENCE QUICKSAND

Fear!

Unfortunately, that next step turned out to be the stuff all her nightmares were made of. There's no sugar-coating it; it was a disaster!

"Before we even opened [to the public], we had an open house for anyone in the community who wanted to come and try it out. Our trial run. It was supposed to be fun," Adelle remembers. "I wanted it to make me feel better about the

Failing!

opening to calm my nerves. Totally the opposite happened. There was a much larger turnout than we expected—we were overwhelmed. We ran out of things, we weren't as prepared as we thought, and it took hours to get the food out. It was very stressful. Definitely wasn't what we were hoping for, at all.

"All night, I kept wishing we had planned everything differently and that we could take it back, start all over. I had to force myself NOT to cry because that wasn't going to help. I wished we could erase the whole horrible night. But you know, that's not how life works. You just have to continue on and learn from it. And actually, we were able to make some changes before we opened for real and then hit the ground running."

Rebounding!

Of course, even after the restaurant opened, it wasn't always smooth sailing. They tried to choose the two days a week they were open carefully. But there were still times when they got way busier than they expected, didn't have enough staff, and had lines out the door.

Adelle worked there as often as she could, but since she was in school, she couldn't always be there. Other times, customers just simply seemed to evaporate, and nobody showed up for days. There was a lot of learning on the job, rolling with it, and plain old trial and error. For somebody who likes to be in control of everything, that uncertainty was stressful.

Here's another thing Adelle couldn't predict: other people's taste. She had to make constant adjustments to the menu, even when it meant other people might like things she didn't. Her personal favorite, the Roma (turkey, Havarti cheese, pesto, and roasted tomatoes) did become the most popular item, but her least favorite, the spicy Buffalo-chicken-and-cheese Fire in the Hole, was a close runner-up.

Adelle actually had to tweak the name of the restaurant, removing the "Ice Cream" part, because she realized that many people had the idea that crepes were only for dessert. She also had to tinker with the hours and days they were open, analyzing sales and numbers to realize that the busiest days are Tuesdays and Saturdays, for lunch and brunch.

Adelle explains, "We've changed almost everything, you know, either a little or a lot, to adapt to what we see working or not working. I decided to stick to more traditional French crepes because I love the French culture and, from the beginning, wanted to bring that to Chattanooga. But also I want to bring some unique crepes that you haven't seen, like Miss America Pie, which is like an apple-pie-based crepe.

"We've swapped in different kinds of waffles, sandwiches and paninis, pastries, and even tried things like soup, which we ended up taking off after a little while. We want to make sure to accommodate as many tastes as possible."

It's also important to her to give back to the community that's supporting her creperie, so she designed "a weekly special, where the proceeds go to different charities. Like during Pride month we ran the Romance special, and we donated 20 percent of the profits to a local charity that helps LGBTQ people that have been kicked out of their homes. Or we've worked with breast cancer support services, March of Dimes, and the Kidney Foundation, too."

By doing it her way, taking this huge project and

managing it step by step, in smaller chunks that she can tackle, Adelle has managed to make her dream a reality. But it can still put a lot of pressure on her. She's set a high standard, and that can quickly become perfectionism. Getting it right, getting it perfect, has often been a goal for her. She knows that's something she has to resist.

"When I was younger, I felt like I had to be perfect in every aspect of life, just to be considered 'good enough.' I put that pressure on myself, but I also felt it from society in general. I had to get the best grades, be the best at soccer, and then when I started the business, I had to make that perfect, too. It seems like to be successful and good at what you do, you have to fit this very specific mold, which feels suffocating."

Dealing with the failures, and then still seeing the business work, learning to keep expectations reasonable, and trusting her gut about how to run the business—all of those have helped Adelle shake the perfectionism and grow into herself. She defines the way she does it, rather than letting anyone else define it for her.

CONFIDENCE
QUICKSAND

People-pleasing!

"My business has definitely helped me be comfortable and feel comfortable in who I am. It allows me to believe that I don't have to find validation from other people and that I'm capable of doing great things.

"Trying to please everyone is ultimately a futile pursuit. You are a lot better and happier being who you are."

Even as she's figured that out, other people make assumptions about her because she's still a teenager. "People ask me," Adelle says, smiling, "if I'm missing out on being a kid and the experience of being young, like I'm denying myself the opportunity to be a kid. The creperie is a huge part of my life and I've been doing it for three years. But to me, I'm redefining what it means to be a kid, I'm just changing what that means to me. I like to get my friends involved in the creperie, too, and a bunch of them have started working there recently. This is my childhood, and I love it. It might not be typical, but it's mine."

Some people just assume that working closely with her mom could be the worst thing ever. Especially for a teenager. But for Adelle, "it actually works great. I love it. She is one of the most hardworking people I've ever met. I grew up watching her start her own company, run it by herself for many years. And she takes that same passion to helping me with this, but still lets me take control and do the work with my vision and doesn't try to trip on that."

Now Adelle is working on ways to expand the creperie, like adding a food truck to go to festivals and events or even park outside hospitals in Chattanooga for staff and patients.

She's also working on a new project, one without crepes. There are a lot of food deserts in

According to the American Nutrition Association, a food desert is an area or neighborhood that doesn't have access to good grocery stores or farmer's markets for healthy fresh fruits and vegetables. People wind up having to shop at quick shops where there's a lot of fast food or junk food.

Chattanooga, places where there are no grocery stores within a mile or more. Originally, she wanted to try to build a grocery store in one of the worst food deserts, which would be a monster of a task. Using what she's learned about adapting, she's creating a plan for a mobile truck-store stocked with healthy food and produce.

When Adelle started, she didn't know any other kids who did what she wanted to do. Now she wants to be the kind of role model she lacked. "My favorite part of all of this is the people I've met, especially kids younger than me. I've had young girls tell me that I'm an inspiration to them, and that meant the world to me. That's definitely been the best part."

JUST Asking

What's your favorite comfort food that makes everything better?

Chicken korma (chicken cooked with spices and yogurt)

What's the one thing that you couldn't live without?

My bike

If you were an animal, what would you be?

A honeybee, because I don't like to stop working or moving

What's the one place you've always wanted to go—your dream destination?

New Zealand

What or who always makes you laugh?

My friends and John Mulaney

What do you like to do on a lazy day?

Don't really like lazy days, but listen to music, read, bike around

CHAPTER 15

Anahi Molano

Sometimes when you try to do something amazing, it can blow up in your face. What seems absolutely incredible in your head can completely fall apart in reality and leave you reeling.

Anahi knows about that, all too well.

"The first time I asked for donations, all my friends and my friends' friends promised to bring tons of clothes. And all sizes, because I didn't want anyone to feel left out. I was so excited. But it totally backfired. The day they were supposed to come, nobody brought anything. NOTHING. It was so humiliating. Oh my God, it was just the worst day."

The "worst day" happened because she'd decided to do something bold and start a thrift shop (a store that sells used clothing) in her school, stocked with donations from everyone she knew. On day one, it flopped, and Anahi was devastated.

After some well-earned tears, though, she realized that maybe she didn't have to just quit. Another option was to dust herself off and come at it a different way. She had total faith in the idea, after all, and she had a strong conviction that "If I'm not going to do it, who is?" So she decided to take another swing at it.

CONFIDENCE BUILDING BLOCK

Rebounding!

The whole thrift store vision had come to her in a flash one day when she was meeting with her principal about school projects. Anahi has always been painfully aware of what it feels like to have the wrong clothes in high school. But in her Mission, Texas, school district, packed with low-income families from the Rio Grande Valley, it's less about being cool and Instagrammable, with a great wardrobe, and more about having something warm to wear when it gets cold.

"It made me more nervous about going to school, especially during the winter, when I had to wear a thin sweater because I was too embarrassed to ask my mother to buy me a jacket when I knew she didn't have the money for it. Instead of focusing in class, I'd be wondering if people noticed I'm wearing what I wore yesterday."

Anahi has also always loved standing up for herself and other people. Looking around the halls of her school, she found herself noticing all the kids who didn't have long-sleeved shirts or sweaters when the temperature dropped or who tried to hide the fact that they wore the same jeans or same sneakers every day. What if it were possible to get all the stuff you truly need, without the pressures of money? Her concept was born.

Anahi's Q&A

What made it seem like a thrift store at school was the best way to help your community?

Poverty is a huge issue within my city, a predominantly low-income Latino community. As a young Hispanic woman from that same background myself, I know how it feels to worry about not having enough clothes to wear to school, or worse, not having the appropriate clothes to match the constantly changing weather.

I go to a school with only four hundred people, so I'm used to seeing the same faces every day. And it's bittersweet watching all these kids I know who clearly can't afford hoodies or jackets in the winter. I know one student in particular who didn't even have a working heater at home. They had to turn on the stove to warm the house, so winter clothes weren't even a possibility. That hit me pretty hard.

Since she wanted to help her fellow students, Anahi hoped to run the thrift shop from the school itself. Of course, that required figuring out lots of details, which is never the fun part! She and her principal decided to use an empty storage room near the school's entrance and ask for donations from all over the community. Instead of money, kids could use vouchers, or tickets, based on merit (like perfect attendance) or their own community service to buy pieces of clothing. One ticket, one piece of clothing.

Now it was time to actually launch the store. The first step was to collect the clothing. Some people like to plan everything out to the teensiest detail, but not Anahi. She likes to jump right in, worried that if she gets bogged down in too many specifics, she will lose steam. Unfortunately, before she'd even gotten a chance to start, she crashed straight into a major bump—that "worst day" ever.

Despite all the promised donations, there was literally nothing. Not one scrap of clothing. Not one donation.

How did you handle that?

CONFIDENCE
BUILDING
BLOCK

Failing!

I felt like nobody was taking my project seriously, like I was a big joke, and it was a huge hit to my confidence. I felt like it was a huge mistake, and I should never have even tried to pull it off in the first place.

When I'm upset I always cry. I just have a huge dramatic crying fit in my room—I had a big one that day. Then I binge-watched my favorite Netflix shows to distract myself. Finally I worked up the courage to look at myself in the mirror and give myself the best pep talk ever, with my Spotify confidence playlist blasting. I told myself that it's perfectly fine to be scared and mess up every once in a while. These things happen.

It was just a test to see whether I'd give up or not, which I didn't.

Here's what's on Anahi's confidence playlist:

"Beautiful" by Christina Aguilera, "Raise Your Glass" by P!nk, "Born This Way" by Lady Gaga, "Irreplaceable" and "Run the World (Girls)" by Beyoncé, "NASA" by Ariana Grande, and "No Scrubs" by TLC.

So what did you do next?

I talked to myself for what seemed to be an hour, before I realized it wasn't the end of the world.

I went back the next day and started over—going into classrooms, this time, and just asking for contributions from everyone beyond just my friends, and it ended up

working pretty well. I had 350 pieces of clothing
when we opened the store.

Once she'd counted and sorted endless T-shirts and
jeans and sweaters and had it all ready to open, Anahi
started to worry about whether kids would actually take
advantage of the store. She knew from experience that
kids can be very hard on themselves and on each other,
so she wanted to set up the thrift store idea as totally fun
and appealing, rather than something embarrassing.

"The biggest issue I've confronted is
shame: kids refuse to speak up, which is
understandable, but it also makes it a lot more
difficult. And help exists, but it's not easy to
combat the shame. I want them to know that it's
just not OK to stay quiet and suffer, when there's
people like me who would love to be their voice."

She knew she needed to get creative about how to
sell the idea of previously owned clothes to her classmates. Then she had a breakthrough. It was a risk, no
question about it. There was a way it could backfire
and Anahi would look ridiculous. And everyone would
know. But she had to try.

So how did you avoid any stigma around donated clothes, especially if your classmates could see people actually shopping for stuff they might have even owned?

Getting the message right was super important. The opportunity to change someone's life lies in every piece of merchandise at the store. I felt like if I opened a thrift store and advertised it as this charity shop for "poor students," my classmates would be way too hesitant to step foot inside. Instead, I promoted it as an environmental sustainability store where recycling clothing would help us practice reuse and sustainability on campus. And that idea appealed to the student body a lot better.

She really hit on something there—that little shift gave the project an entirely different spin. Reduce, reuse, and recycle! It could do all three and help kids at the same time.

And it definitely has been appealing—the store is open three days a week during the year, before school and during the two lunch breaks, with kids flocking to it. The donations keep rolling in, but to keep it fully stocked with lots of sizes and styles, Anahi and her mother have actually been using their own money and shopping to supplement with stuff from a Goodwill or Texas Thrift. People are even talking about taking this idea to other schools in her district.

Donating and buying used clothing is good for the environment because it reduces the amount of waste going into landfills. Most people throw away seventy pounds of clothing a year, according to the World Wear Project. Seventy pounds— that's the weight of the average eleven-year-old! It also takes a lot of energy, chemical dyes, and water to make new clothes, as well as fuel to ship them to stores.

Now that it's a success, do you feel the pressure of more expectations?

It's especially hard for girls and women who want to be professional and also embrace their playful side. Nobody takes us seriously enough to begin with, so I feel like I constantly have to be in CEO mode to please adults, which is draining. I worry I can't get all things right all the time, and I obsess over things kids shouldn't ever have to worry about.

I had this heart-wrenching realization this year that with my schoolwork, I was always trying to impress my teachers, instead of being comfortable with myself. The more pressure I put on myself, the more I didn't want to take risks, the more I was afraid of failing—the less happy I was.

The store, with its failures and successes, has been a petri dish for her to grow her confidence to experiment with just being Anahi . . . with being imperfect sometimes.

What's different now?

I try not to care as much about what other people think! Having the store and having all this contact with so many different adults has really helped. They still treat me with respect, even when I'm being myself.

Just Asking

What's your favorite comfort food
that makes everything better?

Cheeseburgers

What's the one thing that you
couldn't live without?

My dogs

If you were an animal, what would you be?

A Pomeranian

What's the one place you've always wanted
to go—your dream destination?

Japan

What or who always makes you laugh?

Twitter memes

What do you like to do on a lazy day?

Sleep

CHAPTER 16

Thandiwe Abdullah

Ever since she was a little girl, Thandiwe has had an acute awareness of what it means to be black in America and a strong sense of purpose about justice, calling out racial prejudice and trying to end it.

There's a story in Thandiwe's family that she made her first speech at a Mother's Day dinner when she was just six months old, looking around at everybody having fun and toasting the moms, aunts, and grandmas in the room. According to the tale, Thandiwe pulled herself up in her high chair, waved her hand in the air, and babbled something loudly (nobody knew what) to all the folks assembled. Thandiwe was already taking some kind of stand, on something, even that early on, and her family thinks that's when her passion for activism all started. BOOM.

Thandiwe could hardly have imagined that thirteen years later, she'd help launch an antiracist youth movement.

She started her first campaign in elementary school by forming an organization with a bunch of her friends called the Junior Freedom Fighters. They had a very ambitious three-point plan: end all wars, save the environment, and shut down poverty.

"It was so silly," she remembers now. "We had such huge goals and we thought we could do them! We just went around talking to other kids and then we had a protest in our local park, where we were marching around saying stuff like, 'homelessness is bad, war's bad.' But," she laughs, "we did get people from the community to come out."

And if you're an activist, getting people out into the streets is always a great start!

Then came an event that totally cemented her feeling that using her voice and standing up for what she believes is the path for her.

At ten years old, Thandiwe traveled with her mother

from California to Ferguson, Missouri, to take part in protests after unarmed teenager Michael Brown was killed by a cop. Marching in the streets, she witnessed sharp divisions between the mourners and the police, and even outright violent confrontations. The life-and-death costs of racial injustice became very clear to her. Afterward, she was definitely upset.

"I was thinking that it's not safe for me to be out here doing this, but I want to be," she says. "So after that, I was kind of focused on finding a safer way, a more youth-friendly way, to organize, because there's not a lot of outlets for young people to get to say what they need to say, to get it off their chests."

Since there wasn't that kind of opportunity for kids, Thandiwe decided to create one.

During the next year, she worked hard to put together a weeklong summer day camp for other kids with an interest in fighting racism, stopping racial stereotyping, and becoming activists. Working with Black Lives Matter activists in Los Angeles, Thandiwe thought about how to make the whole week fun and rewarding, plus useful and productive, so she spent months talking to all kinds of different people, like local community groups and organizations that help kids.

She put flyers up in her school and had friends put them up at their schools. Thandiwe asked adults to help her post them on social media so that people could sign up from all over LA, where she lives. She also reached out to other summer camps to partner with them for part of each day, so that she could include as many different kids as possible.

When the camp happened that next summer, it turned out to be better than she'd hoped. She remembers, "It was fun. We had a delicious breakfast, then people came in to do yoga with us. We sat in poetry and hip-hop circles, getting to express ourselves and our hopes and fears. And we learned a lot about the civil rights struggle. We even went over media training, know-your-rights training, and self-defense training, which is all good to know if you are trying to be an activist."

Rather than waiting for someone else to come up with a cool place for young activists to get started—Thandiwe went out and made it. That made her feel strong. And that could have been enough. Sometimes you do something that's just amazing on its own. That week of camp definitely was. Other times, you do something amazing that leads to something else amazing. That week of camp definitely did that, too.

She thinks that the seeds of everything she does now grew from that camp. Thandiwe made her next move in middle school. She became cofounder of the **Black Lives Matter Youth Vanguard**, working with Black Lives Matter in Schools, pushing for racial justice in education.

The group worked with the teachers' union, parents, school administrators, and other people in communities all over the country, advocating for changes that would make the school experience more fair, safe, and equal for people of color. Banding together, they created a blueprint. It called for equality in the way students are disciplined, mandated black history and ethnic studies, and asked for more funding for counselors and more black teachers. It was adopted by the National Education Association.

There were four main themes of the blueprint: end "zero tolerance" discipline and implement restorative justice; hire more black teachers; mandate black history and ethnic studies in K–12 curriculum; and fund counselors, not cops.

Next up, Thandiwe and Black Lives Matter in Schools worked with another organization, **LA Students**

Deserve, to rally a wide-ranging community of kids and teachers and parents against what they believe to be one of the worst examples of stereotyping and unfair treatment in the LA schools: racially profiling black and brown kids and targeting them with random searches.

Thandiwe told us what it's like when those searches happen. Imagine a security guard, school administrator, or uniformed police officer suddenly opens the door during one of your classes.

"Random searches start in middle school. I've experienced it since the sixth grade and it's a traumatizing experience. They come in right in the middle of class, interrupting the whole lesson, pick you out in front of all your friends, all your peers, and your teacher, and then they say, 'Come with me.' And then you get wanded down (using a metal detector). You feel that you have no privacy, and they dump all your stuff from your bag on the ground and look through it."

She went on to explain why she feels these searches are singling out the kids of color. "My school has a heavily white and Asian population. If you look around in my classroom, there's only four or five black students in the classroom. And yet somehow, when the searches happen, all four or five of us are being taken out. What does that say?"

The LA teachers' union, the American Civil Liberties Union, and parent organizations all agreed and started to intensely pressure the LA school board to stop these searches. Recently, the school board actually abolished the policy. Thandiwe was totally overjoyed!

Now fifteen, Thandiwe feels proud to have taken part in this change. Of course, there's no shortage of other issues for her to tackle, including a do-rag ban at her school and the police violence against black and brown people in this country.

CONFIDENCE BUILDING BLOCK

Resilience!

Do-rags, in case you don't know, are scarves wrapped tightly around the head, sometimes under other caps, worn mostly by people of color.

But she also knows something important—you have to savor the victories when they come. Not getting overwhelmed or bogged down with expectations of getting everything perfect (including herself!) is absolutely essential to being able to keep trying, take risks, and build up your confidence stockpile.

She's also not afraid to say that she needs plenty of help and support. On top of her activism, she's a diligent student with tons of interests, so she says, "I founded a group because I don't want to do everything. I'm not trying to do it all by myself.

"In our organization, we don't have just one leader—we all have the power to take action. I can say, 'Hey, I can't do this. I'm really stressed out or I'm tired and I just had finals and I need someone else to take over . . .'"

When she does get stressed, or anxious, or even afraid, she likes to quote a line from *After Earth*, a Will and Jaden Smith movie that she loves. "Fear is a choice." She explains, "Fear is something that exists in your head, you create it. It's a product of your imagination that causes you to focus on hypothetical, irrational things. Fear is not a real thing. Danger is a real thing. So why not do something about the danger that is causing you to fear?"

And Thandiwe also reminds herself of something her mother told her. "She said to walk with purpose, which means whatever you choose:

Do it with purpose.

I just feel like this is my purpose, being an activist for racial justice. That's the path I decided to go on, so I'm doing it with purpose."

JUST ASKING

What's your favorite comfort food
that makes everything better?

Baked mac and cheese

What's the one thing that you
couldn't live without?

Books

If you were an animal, what would you be?

A giraffe

What's the one place you've always wanted
to go—your dream destination?

Morocco or Brazil

What or who always makes you laugh?

SpongeBob memes

What do you like to do on a lazy day?

Read a book, eat ice cream, drink tea

CHAPTER 17

Dexa

exa has listened to the radio her whole life. Everyone she knows is glued to it—more than television. It's the main source for political news, cricket and soccer games, even health information.

So recently when she had the opportunity to actually *be* on the radio, she was overwhelmed. Dexa sat in the studio, staring at the radio microphone, knowing that her voice was about to ring out all over rural Nepal. She was especially worried that her voice would sound different—most of the voices she's ever heard on the radio have been male. Girls' and womens'

CONFIDENCE BUILDING BLOCK

Risk!

voices are hardly ever there.

But sixteen-year-old Dexa was asked to host a program on October 11, the International Day of the Girl, because she had something important to say. And she knew, whether her voice was different or not, she had to use it to make change. Her female voice wouldn't be the only hard thing to hear: her subject was controversial. She was there to tackle the stigma around periods so that more girls in Nepal could get to go to school.

Too many girls in Nepal regularly miss school or drop out entirely once they hit puberty because of the stigma of menstruation. Dexa experienced some of that herself. She's taken this on as her battle to fight because, as she says, "Education can help girls fulfill their dreams and end injustice, so parents must allow their daughters access! If girls are treated equally they can do anything that boys can do."

You'll remember reading about period empowerment and #freeperiods in Amika's chapter. In Dexa's story, you can see the same issue through the eyes of someone living with its consequences in daily life.

Dexa's Q&A

How did you first realize that girls are held back by the fact that they have periods, a plain old fact of biology that they can't control? When did it hit you?

I live in Parbat, Gandaki Province, a rural part of Nepal. The majority of people there are Hindu and tend to be pretty conservative. When I entered puberty, I cried my heart out because my grandmother told me I couldn't go to school for eleven days and had to remain isolated for twenty-one days without seeing the sun, my father, or any male members of my family. I was shocked.

In the traditional Hindu culture in Nepal, girls had to retreat to tiny huts called "goths" during their periods because they were considered impure. But through education and programs like World Menstrual Hygiene Day (menstrualhygieneday.org), things are changing.

Then it got worse. She also told me I couldn't even touch my books for seven days.

Fortunately, my father objected. My parents are teachers and value education. So I didn't have to miss school, but there were other restrictions about socializing with people or doing certain things. During my periods, for instance, I'm ousted from the kitchen for four days. In the beginning, I was so embarrassed that everyone knew.

Dexa recognized that if this was happening to her, it was even harder for the girls whose parents were more traditional. Looking around in her classroom, this was painfully clear.

What was happening at your school, once girls started to hit puberty?

In my village, people think that since girls are sent to their husband's home eventually, they should learn household chores rather than going to school. Getting an education is a secondary thing for them.

I could count the number of actively participating and engaged girls on both hands. Girls were always behind the boys, but

I wanted them in the front row! They were kind of aimless, with no expectations for their futures. They also had very little accurate knowledge about health and hygiene. They thought their periods were a curse from God. They'd miss school every month and didn't know anything about sanitary products.

Dexa herself was passionate about school, and she felt bad for her friends and classmates, especially the younger girls, who were missing out. In ninth grade, she went to a program at school run by Plan International. Paging through the brochures they brought, she saw all sorts of cool programs started by girls around the world. BING! A light-bulb moment: she'd start one, too!

Dexa began working on an awareness campaign about period health for her village school. As she says, "The program was all about making girls and their parents aware about menstrual hygiene and reproductive health along with the taboos associated with it."

Once she figured out the *what* of her idea, she had to figure out the *how*.

Where did you start?

First I searched through the web for ways to convince girls not to be ashamed of menstruation or of themselves. I asked for guidance from my parents, teachers, and other students.

After collecting lots of ideas, I started working on a plan. I always spend a lot of time on a good plan, because good planning means the work is halfway done already when you finally start. Then all the rest is just doing it. It wasn't as easy as I thought it would be. Sometimes I was exhausted and wanted to give up, but my parents encouraged me to keep working.

So, what did you come up with?

I prepared pamphlets to teach these girls about the whole female reproductive system and the menstrual cycle. I wanted girls to see that it was natural and not a punishment or a reason to be looked down upon.

I asked some friends to join me in leading discussion groups at school using the pamphlets. There were about fifteen to twenty girls. We talked a lot about role models, like Malala. And it turned out many of the girls dreamed of becoming nurses, if they could stay in school, so I pointed to Florence Nightingale and Madame Curie. I also told them about Junko Tabei, the first woman to summit Mount Everest, and Benazir Bhutto, first female prime minister of Pakistan.

Narrow-minded people think that girls cannot do anything. But I showed the girls that we've already proven that we can do anything.

CONFIDENCE QUICKSAND

Stereotyping!

We just tried to emphasize that message. At first, girls were reluctant, but we made them feel comfortable and got them to share their feelings. And we showed them some sample sanitary products. We also had taken donations to make sure that we could stock supplies at the school. Some girls had never seen a pad before!

overthinking!

Dexa was happy with her sessions with the girls, at first. Then she realized that she hadn't factored in an important piece of this puzzle: the parents. Uh-oh. She started to have massive doubts. While the girls had been frightened, but open, Dexa understood that their parents could be the bigger obstacle. They could control whether the girls were allowed to attend school at all, or were able to participate in more discussions. She couldn't expect girls to do it alone. And changing adults' mind-sets is harder than convincing more flexible-thinking kids.

But then Dexa used a strategy she always pulls out to control her negative thoughts.

What is this strategy?

When I am scared or face a risk, I just remind myself of my original determination. And I say "BMW"—bless my work—to gain courage and confidence. If that doesn't work, I also tell myself, "OK, try one last time and you are done. You can quit." Once I do it one last time, I usually want to do it again. Thoughts like "Nothing is working out" cross my mind all the time. They could stop me, but I try to remember the enthusiasm I had when I started. That usually works.

Since parents were usually the source of the attitudes about periods, how did you decide to approach them?

The girls themselves weren't ready to talk to their parents, so we had to reach them. Talking with my own parents, we came up with the idea of getting to parents during parent-teacher meetings.

We made presentations to them about the problems and limitations their daughters face when they are just confined within the four walls of home during their periods. And we told them the science about the health hazards and risks for girls who neglect or don't understand the importance of hygiene.

At first, we could not convince them. There were some people who accused us of going against their traditional values and religion. It was difficult to change that kind of mind-set, both in the girls and their parents.

It was slow going and frustrating. But after about a year, she started to see improvement. The shift in the parents' thinking, and the girls', has actually had stunning results.

What's changed for the girls you know?

Nowadays, no girl at my school misses a day because of her period.

Parents have become more conscious about their daughters' studies. Girls now confidently put their views forth without inhibition. We have even made them the new coordinators of this campaign so that they can teach other young girls!

Dexa is aware that this message has to go broader

to touch more girls. Hers is just one school with a very small number of girls and families. Still, she learned that education works. Big time.

What do you think needs to happen next, to open opportunities for girls?

For so many years, there's been no investment in girls. There's a traditional saying, "Where the women are worshipped, gods dwell there." Yet we are underestimated. Most of the girls in the country are still dropouts, as they get married early and have no independence. We need to stop that cycle.

That's why Dexa was so honored to host that radio show on the International Day of the Girl. It was the first step toward her dream of being a journalist and another opportunity to spread important information. With one shot at this airtime, she wanted it to be powerful.

Growing up listening to the radio nonstop, what was it like to know that your own voice was in homes all over Nepal?

It was an overwhelming feeling. I wanted to make sure that topics about girls that are usually overlooked got attention, like gender discrimination, women's empowerment, girls' participation in politics, and skill trainings for girls.

If I were to hear other girls or women on the radio, I'd want to join them and **bring voice to the voiceless.** So that's what I was able to do—and intend to keep doing!

---

* We aren't using her real name to protect her identity, as her work is still controversial in Nepal. So we are calling her Dexa, which means "to teach."

Just Asking

What's your favorite comfort food that makes everything better?

Yogurt

What's the one thing that you couldn't live without?

Self-respect

If you were an animal, what would you be?

A dog

What's the one place you've always wanted to go—your dream destination?

The Karnali region of Nepal

What or who always makes you laugh?

The happiness of other people

What do you like to do on a lazy day?

Read novels

CHAPTER 18

Autumn Peltier

utumn has spent her whole life surrounded by water. She's grown up on Manitoulin Island, the largest freshwater island in the world. It sits in the middle of Lake Huron, and next to Georgian Bay and the North Channel, in northern Ontario, Canada. Her island has huge rivers dividing it, and over a hundred lakes. And some of those lakes are connected to little lakes meandering off in all directions. She's always had a deep connection to the natural beauty and the water around her. Still, she never expected to turn into a water protector, traveling all over the world to defend the importance of pure water and its essential place in our lives.

Autumn is a member of the Eagle Clan Anishinaabe-kwe and of the Wikwemikong First Nation, and she's always been taught by her elders that water itself has a spirit, that it is precious. The name of the island, Manitoulin, comes from an indigenous word for spirit; a spirit said to live in its caves. With the bountiful fresh water on Manitoulin, she grew up on the reserve seeing water, or *nibi*, as a life force.

In Canada, the indigenous people who have lived there for thousands of years are called First Nations.

"We believe our water is sacred," Autumn explained to us, "because we are born of water and live in water (in our mother's womb) for nine months. When the water breaks, new life comes. But even deeper than that, we come from our mother's water, and her mother's water, and so on.

Autumn's work is similar to that of Melati and Isabel, from the beginning of the book, who are protecting the ocean across the world in Bali!

All the original water flows through us from the beginning and all around us."

She just assumed everyone else felt that way, too. But when she was about eight years old, she started to notice that maybe everyone didn't share her beliefs. Waterways in her area were becoming contaminated, from oil pipelines and boat traffic. Where she lives, Autumn could still drink the water. But in neighboring towns, people were boiling their drinking water because it was so polluted. And that pollution was way more common on reserves, where indigenous people like Autumn lived, than in other areas. She was both a little mad and a little scared. How could that happen? Who would let it? And what could she do?

As it turned out, she had an incredible role model for how to take action right in front of her. Autumn's aunt, Josephine Mandamin, had been protesting the growing contamination of all the lakes and rivers and streams since the early 2000s, working with a group called the Mother Earth Water Walk. As a way to call attention to the threat to water, she and other women walked the shorelines of the Great Lakes every spring for years, eventually trekking over seventeen thousand miles!

Inspired by her aunt, Autumn decided to be her own kind of water advocate, a water warrior. Maybe she wouldn't take those long marches (that seemed intimidating), but she could use her voice. She started small, by writing a speech about water in the Ojibwa/Odawa dialect of Anishinaabe, for an assignment. Other kids seemed to listen to her, and she thought she might be the right person to get this message across.

She started to speak at different community gatherings. After a couple of years, she got invited to the Children's Climate Conference in Stockholm, Sweden, and to the Special Chiefs Assembly meeting of the Assembly of First Nations (a group that represents many indigenous people in Canada) in Ottawa. At the Assembly meeting, she presented Canadian prime minister Justin Trudeau with a traditional copper water bowl to remind him to protect the water and told him tearfully that she "wasn't happy with the choices he'd made and the broken promises to [her] people."

That was a pretty big deal. What's it like to be twelve years old and telling adults what to do about the planet? She was definitely nervous and remembers being jittery, but she remembers her stronger feeling: "Saving the water is the right thing, it's a really good thing."

After these trips, Autumn went back to spending most of her time doing normal kid things, like going to school, doing her homework, and making slime with her sister. And then she got a big invitation: to speak at the United Nations in New York City, launching the International Decade for Action on Water for Sustainable Development on World Water Day. Having seen news coverage about her, UN officials wanted Autumn's unique perspective for this day dedicated to water.

For tons of reasons, it almost didn't happen. First of all, the emailed invitation for her to speak went to her mom's email, and her mom assumed it was a joke. It wasn't. Fortunately, they figured that out. Then to get to New York City from Manitoulin Island, Autumn, her mom, and the chief of her community set off on their journey: a long car trip to Toronto, then a four a.m. flight from there. But then all flights were canceled because of winter weather.

Was that the end? People from Canada stopped by some snow in New York? No way! Her chief looked her in the eye and asked if she absolutely wanted to get there, even if it meant driving all night. She knew it was the chance of a lifetime, so she nodded. Back in the car they went, arriving at the UN with just moments to spare.

CONFIDENCE BUILDING BLOCK

ME TO WE Thinking!

Nerves? Not this time. She left them at home, hours and hours before. "I felt a lot of confidence at that moment," she says, "because I was standing up for my people. It's not only my message but everyone else's message as well."

Speaking from the heart, the thirteen-year-old told leaders at the UN, "I have taken a photo of where we are today with various issues surrounding our water. My snapshot doesn't look good in terms of pollution, climate change, pipelines breaking, recycling, sanitation, poverty, hunger, and illnesses related to these issues. One day, I will be an ancestor and I want my great-grandchildren to know that I tried hard to fight so they can have clean drinking water."

And then she said something so powerful that we can't stop thinking about it:

"Now's the time to warrior up. And empower each other to take a stand for our planet."

Facing world leaders, as crazy as it sounds, wasn't hard for Autumn, because after those earlier events, her confidence had grown. But back at home, she faced a new challenge. Autumn had stood up for something she believed in, publicly, and not everyone agreed with her that the water needs so much protecting. People started to bully her. Autumn was bullied so badly that, at one point, her mom pulled her out of school for a while. Kids were pushing her and actually throwing things at her face.

Somehow her message about protecting the water made her a target, not just for kids, but for adults, too. She didn't want to be around anyone or see anybody. And it wasn't just at school—it happened online, too. Social media makes her feel very vulnerable, even intimidated. When it got bad, Autumn felt like quitting her water activism.

Luckily, a counselor helped her to cope with it, teaching Autumn some mental games to be able to calm down, focus, and talk herself back from whirling thoughts and brain-spinning

CONFIDENCE QUICKSAND

Overthinking!

fears. Her mom was super supportive, and her friends kept her mind off it whenever they could by going for walks with her, listening to music, or playing with her dog.

Autumn has definitely learned that if she wants to do what she believes in, she won't please everyone all the time. It's OK if some people don't like her message. She's learned to be very cautious with social media and not pay it much attention. With hard work and lots of help, she's gotten to a place where she can ignore bullies, stay strong, and do what she thinks is right.

CONFIDENCE BUILDING BLOCK

Resilience!

And now Autumn needs to take on even more responsibility. Her aunt Josephine fell ill and, before she died, she asked Autumn to carry on her work, to be the next "her." Autumn feels like she's now learned enough to do it. The Anishinabek Nation, a political advocacy group for forty First Nations across Ontario, named Autumn as the chief water commissioner, following in her aunt's footsteps. She's already had some good news: the Canadian government has promised that by 2021, the tap water all over Canada should be clean enough for drinking and there won't be any more "boiled-water advisories."

There's a lot more to do, though, to nourish the water around her back to health. More people to talk to, more places to go, more ways to honor the spirit of water. Autumn says she's ready to **"WARRIOR UP."**

Just Asking

What's your favorite comfort food
that makes everything better?

Pizza

What's the one thing that you
couldn't live without?

My dog

If you were an animal, what would you be?

An orca whale

What's the one place you've always wanted
to go—your dream destination?

Hawaii

What or who always makes you laugh?

My mom

What do you like to do on a lazy day?

Watch Netflix

CHAPTER 19

Natália Pereira

Ten-year-old Natália Pereira, who goes by Nati, just wants to play soccer. Nati lives in Santa Catarina, Brazil, a country with an awesome soccer tradition. Ever heard of Pelé, known as the King of Futbol? He's one of the most famous players of all time, and he's from Brazil. One of the best national women's teams is also in Brazil. It's definitely the national sport; it's practically in the air the kids breathe, the water they drink.

Nati has played since she was four, running, dribbling, dodging—she can do it all for hours and hours on end. She's known for her flawless feint, a soccer move where she fakes out her opponent about where she's going with the ball. But she wasn't getting to use her skills much on the pitch because she didn't have a real team for herself. In Santa Catarina, there are no girls' teams. None. That's the kind of thing that could have put a stop to Nati's passion for soccer. A setback like that could have ended her soccer dreams. But it didn't. In fact, it made her even more single-minded.

No girls' team? Fine. Nati would play with the boys and beat them, too.

For this book of real stories we asked Rose Lavelle, US National Team player, 2019 Women's World Cup Champion, professional soccer player with the Washington Spirit, and one of the most creative, hardworking soccer players today, to nominate a confident girl. She chose Nati Pereira.

"I recognized Nati's drive and determination instantly. Nati built her confidence by ignoring obstacles, channeling her passion for the game. In the face of being told no regularly, Nati just put her head down and worked. When it looked like there was no place for her, she was resolute and *made* room for herself."

After a while, Nati decided to try out for the youth academy of a professional league, called Avaí. She'd be the only girl in the whole country on that kind of team. Of course, that didn't stop her!

=GOAL=

KICK

She practiced four days a week, worked really hard, and made it!

"It's very cool to be on a real team... If we miss a pass, everyone says, 'It's OK, come on, let's go.' It's kind of a second family."

Nati's so eager to play that she looks for even more ways to challenge herself. Poking around online, she found Centro Olímpico, a team of top girl players in São Paulo.

"There were a ton of pictures of them winning championships, so I knew that they were really good! I talked my mom into taking me to try out for them, even though it was almost 500 miles away. I made that team, too!"

"So now I play with Centro Olímpico once a month, even though I have to fly there and miss some school. The girls are from all over the country and it's awesome."

She won't be able to play with the boys forever. So Nati's making sure to grab every opportunity that comes her way, like when she was invited to play with American girls for an exhibition in Orlando, Florida.

"These girls on the under-fourteen team in Orlando were GIANTS. But it was cool!"

Nati! Nati! Nati! Nati! Nati!

"I just played my game with them, the only way I know how. By the end, their moms were all calling my name!"

"When I started playing, my mom made me wear a bow on the field, tso she could spot me easily."

"As soon as I got home, I ripped that bow off."

"Then my mother would put it back on. Put it back on. Put it on. Put it on. Put it on."

Nati discovered a great confidence strategy: finding a little lucky charm that helps you stay calm when your brain is about to start spinning.

"Now I never play without it. One time we were almost at a game, all the way across the bridge, when I made my dad turn around. I said, 'Dad, go back! I forgot my bow!' Otherwise, I couldn't play."

"And it makes me feel less scared when traveling. Or going places where I don't know the language. But when I feel like people out there know me, it's better."

One incredible thing Nati has discovered is the power of being present, the ability to stay focused, tune out all distractions, and really tap into a state of flow.

"Once I start to play, I'm determined and confident. I don't think about anything else and I trust that I'm going to know what to do. Kick, dribble, run..."

Her state of flow is also a state of pure confidence. And that's an important lesson for everyone!

CHAPTER 20

Gitanjali Rao

Gitanjali has a notebook that she fills with ideas. Her ideas usually have to do with ions, binding molecules, decreasing current flow, conductivity, or other cool science stuff. She uses it like a sketchbook for science daydreaming.

Gitanjali's uncle gave her a science kit when she was three years old and she became, in a word, obsessed. She loved the idea of making things change colors with different chemical reactions or causing crystals to dissolve. She turned basically everything that happened to her into one mini-experiment or another, constantly exploring a theory or setting up a pop-up laboratory in her room. She remembers it as almost an addiction.

So, when eleven-year-old Gitanjali heard about the water crisis in Flint, Michigan, where over a hundred thousand people were being exposed to lead contamination in their drinking water, she was absolutely positive that there'd be an answer in science. And she set out to come up with it.

That wasn't a huge leap for her to take. Since kindergarten she'd worked on her own inventions from scratch. By second grade, for example, she was dreaming up a chair that could flip under the floor when nobody needed it, but would pop back up into the room when someone wanted a seat. She was picturing it for small contained spaces, like the International Space Station. Even for normal rooms, it could eliminate clutter. That never really took off. But it didn't stop her from dreaming and imagining and inventing.

The next year, when she was eight years old, she developed something she called My Intuition, which was a set of tools for people with different disabilities. She was working on glasses that would translate visual information to people who can't see, or a wristwatch that would convert sounds into a written description for people who can't hear and would also read text out loud when typed by people who can't speak. Those didn't really work either. But since her favorite part of science is having the opportunity to try different ways of solving real-life problems, she just kept going. And in science, you have to be willing to fail a lot of the time, to figure out what works.

CONFIDENCE
BUILDING
BLOCK

Failing!

When she learned about the situation in Flint, she was shocked. Even though she lives far away in Colorado, she found it upsetting.

"It was appalling and unfair that people didn't have clean water to drink. I took it for granted every day. It bothered me that so many kids my age were being affected," she says. "It just didn't seem right that children would have to drink lead-contaminated water. It affects them the most, because kids are still growing. On top of the nausea, the headaches, and the rashes caused by lead, kids' growing bones will absorb it like it's calcium. And that causes more damage." The issue of lead-contaminated water is way bigger than just one American city—it's happening all over the world, including India, where Gitanjali has a lot of family.

At first, she didn't know how to solve this, but since she believes that science can hold all the answers, she dived into research. She told us,

"When I see a problem, I drill it into my brain. Then I start reading and poking around for ideas."

CONFIDENCE
BUILDING
BLOCK

Resilience!

At the beginning, she was focusing on a way to remove the lead from the water, but not coming up with much inspiration. Her parents always encouraged her to think outside the box, so she tried it from another angle—what about concentrating on detecting the lead in the water first, before anyone uses it? That way you don't necessarily treat the problems caused by the toxic water; instead you try to limit any exposure to it in the first place. Obviously, the water shouldn't have lead in it at all, but she was tackling one problem at a time.

One day she was reading an article on the website of the Massachusetts Institute of Technology about using carbon nanotube sensors to detect hazardous gas in the air, when she realized that she could adapt that to work with liquid. A liquid like water. Bam!

She pictured a portable device about the size of a walkie-talkie powered by a nine-volt battery with a thin strip of sensors along a wand to dip in the water and read the level of lead. But that was just the first step. She was determined to make it easy to understand so that anybody could use it. Gitanjali wanted the results of the sensor's reading of the water quality to be sent straight to a device that's already in hand: a smartphone. Device + app = big undertaking for Gitanjali.

163 million people in India don't have access to safe water. As Gitanjali says in her 2018 Tedx talk, "fifteen million children in developing countries suffer from lead poisoning, one hundred thousand water systems in India have lead contamination, and 33 percent (a third) of water samples from the top twenty-six cities in India have harmful levels of lead."

She was definitely a little intimidated about tackling such a project. Even though inventing and experimenting comes naturally to her, she was still in the dark about how this would work, what would happen, and how she could make this concept a reality. A science competition, the Discovery Education 3M Young Scientist Challenge, gave her the push she needed to actually build and test her idea. And for inspiration, she looked to Marie Curie, one of the only female role models in science that she knows. And Karlie Kloss, a supermodel who codes. She liked the idea that you can combine different talents to create something totally unexpected and totally unique.

An eleven-year-old trying something so ambitious was unexpected. One of the biggest hurdles was simply finding a place to work, coming up with a lab that would allow a young girl to do all the tests involving carbon nanotubes, chloride, and lead acetate, because nobody took her seriously. They thought she was a cute kid with a cute little science project, but that is not how she ever saw herself. She had to be extremely determined to just get this phase off the ground. There were so many calls, emails, and boring follow-up things to do. But proving that she *could* do it was important. With a lot of help from all kinds of people, she entered her invention, a device called Tethys (named for the Greek goddess of fresh water), into the competition. And she won!

Actually, she won twice that year, first the Young Scientist award and then the EPA's President's

Environmental Youth Award. So clearly those judges think that her invention has incredible potential to help improve lives. They awarded her prize money to research and fine-tune her idea even further. Working with professional scientists at Denver Water, Gitanjali is still testing all the many possibilities for errors and false positives (like Tethys reading the fluoride in most American drinking water as a hazardous chemical) to get it foolproof.

She also wants to figure out a way for Tethys to be made on a large scale and sold to people all over the world. She thinks it can be used in schools and homes, since it's hard to tell exactly where water comes from and what pipes it travels through to get to faucets and drinking fountains. She's passionate about being a scientist and an inventor, but she is also interested in the business side of her invention, so that it can be available, at a low, affordable cost, to all the people who need it. As much as she loves the creative role, it won't mean as much if it doesn't reach the people she wants to help.

Along the way, she learned something else about herself: she likes to compete and likes to win. And that's a good thing because it pushes her to take risks, tackle challenges, and not give up when she fails. Gitanjali is not shy about saying that the desire to beat her competition helped motivate her. She's irritated that she keeps running into gender stereotypes in science, like the fact that she's often been the only girl at a STEM camp. "So imagine all the other girls who are kind of just easing their way into science but being the only girl in the classroom, feeling uncomfortable," she remembers. "It's just sad that stuff like this can happen even in this day and age."

CONFIDENCE
QUICKSAND

stereotyping!

Speaking of real-world situations that should not still be happening, Gitanjali is also outspoken about the gender pay gap—the difference between what men and women earn doing the same job. Sometimes she can't believe it's still common, but her beloved research tells her that it definitely is. And she knows it makes no sense. "It's just plain dumb. Women should always get paid the same amount as the guy doing the same job."

Even with these issues, Gitanjali believes in what she's doing and keeps her eyes focused on what drives her. "For me, it's not just science. I love science. But I also love this journey that science is taking me on."

Just Asking

What's your favorite comfort food that makes everything better?

Deep-fried French toast

What's the one thing that you couldn't live without?

Music

If you were an animal, what would you be?

A dolphin

What's the one place you've always wanted to go—your dream destination?

The Galápagos Islands or Madagascar

What or who always makes you laugh?

Inside jokes and dad jokes

What do you like to do on a lazy day?

Eat cookie-dough ice cream and binge TV

CHAPTER 21

Angelina Tropper

When she was younger, eleven-year-old Angelina would get a knot in the pit of her stomach as she'd head to school. Not the way we all feel when we didn't study for a test or finish a project, or when we totally hate what we're wearing, or we've had a fight with a friend. Each day as she walked through the doors, Angelina felt that her deepest, darkest secret might be exposed. School seemed harder for her than for the other kids, and she was sure there was something wrong with her.

As much as she loved reading, Angelina couldn't quite finish a book. She had trouble copying from the board accurately, and math, as she says, "forget about it!" Yet all along, she kept it to herself. It's hard to be yourself when you are hiding a big part of you; keeping secrets is a big burden. So she was unhappy and scared.

Then when she was nine years old, her parents had her tested, and it turns out that her brain just works differently. She has a learning disability and ADHD. With extra help, she started to feel a lot better about school. But she still wanted to keep it a secret. It was embarrassing and made her feel vulnerable and different.

One day, after she heard a friend confess her own embarrassing secret, Angelina decided enough was enough. She told her friends, and it felt good. She realized it was time to be

You may recognize that Angelina's got a challenge similar to Ciara-Beth and Greta, but not identical. For some people, autism can mean that they are super focused, and ADHD can mean that it's a bit harder to harness their thoughts. So, like them, Angelina had to figure out how to best work with her unique brain!

honest about it in a bigger way, because it could help other people to feel less alone. It's easier for Angelina to explain everything in writing, so she poured her story into a blog post, which the Malala Fund wound up publishing!

Now she can help tons of other kids, just by embracing what she thought was a shameful weakness and sharing her vulnerability.

Angelina's Q&A

What was it like before you knew what was going on, when you were keeping this secret?

I was actually going through a rough time, but nobody around me knew. At school, I had to work more than everyone else. I would forget things super fast, even chores at home. I didn't do it on purpose, but people thought I was lazy or didn't want to listen. I would forget choreographies during ballet lessons, I had trouble studying, I couldn't read at the speed that my friends could, and I couldn't write full sentences.

It was weird: if I sat with my mom, for example, doing homework, like writing a paragraph, I could say it perfectly. But as soon as I would write it down exactly like I thought I said it, my mom would point out: "Hey, you forgot to finish the sentence, or you forgot a word here..." My brain would think that I wrote it down, but in real life I hadn't. So I was worried. I didn't know how to tell anyone. I was afraid.

At school, I was also having trouble just copying from the board. I would skip lines or words and when my teachers would ask me if I understood something, I would just say that I did. See, for you it is probably the easiest thing to just copy something, but for me it isn't. It is hard for me to focus on lines when I am reading and often I skip letters, words, or even sentences.

CONFIDENCE
QUICKSAND

overthinking!

I didn't want to call attention to myself. I decided to pretend that everything was OK, and it worked for a while. But then I started getting overwhelmed and scared of failing. I started having nightmares, sleepless nights, and severe anxiety episodes.

So, then what happened?

My parents and my teacher noticed. I ended up getting a psychological educational assessment and I was diagnosed with a learning disability and ADHD. Hearing the doctors say that I had done really well in the tests and that nothing was wrong with me was amazing. They explained that my brain was wired differently and that I had to find new ways of learning. I literally felt like a bunch of rocks were taken off my back.

Did everything suddenly get better? Was it like a magic _whoosh_ and all your problems went away?

Well, my parents and I were happy because at least now I knew that I could keep on trying and studying the new way. But I still tried to keep my struggles secret, especially around my friends and at school. I refused to get some additional help that I was supposed to because I didn't want people to see me going into special ed classes. I was afraid of being made fun

CONFIDENCE QUICKSAND

People-pleasing!

of or being seen as stupid.

I had seen bullying in my school toward kids with learning disabilities or mental health conditions, and I was afraid that that would happen to me, too. At the same time I was tired of pretending and wanted to speak up.

Months before this, Angelina and her friends created **Care Gift Elves**, a group that tries to spread kindness by doing things like taking gifts to families in homeless shelters or organizing cleanups of the beaches around Lake Ontario, near where she lives in Toronto, Canada. That experience was already helping her see how much she enjoys getting involved and making a difference in other people's lives. Then, one day, everything came together for her.

How did that help encourage you to open up about your learning disability?

Once, during a Care Gift Elves meeting, one of my friends shared a very personal story about struggling with courage in school. It inspired me and made me come out of my shell. So I decided to write about what it is like to be a girl in fifth grade with a learning disability and ADHD in a blog. I thought that if I had time to put my thoughts together and write them down, I would be able to explain it better and make kids and adults understand what it is like. I was just tired of not being able to be myself.

Did that seem scary?

To be honest, I jumped right in, like jumping into a pool of really cold water. I think it's better to just do it so you don't have time to change your mind.

CONFIDENCE
BUILDING
BLOCK

Risk!

Then my blog post about my learning disability was published by the Malala Fund newsletter, Assembly! Seeing my story in the middle of all those other inspiring girls and knowing that what I wrote was important enough for such a cool site was amazing. I finally felt heard. When people even commented and reached out from all these different countries, I saw that my blog post had made a difference.

What about the reaction from kids at school?

It wasn't as bad as I thought. All of my friends were nice and supportive. I do sometimes get comments making fun of my learning disability. It bothers me, but I am learning to brush them off. I know that there are always going to be people who feel the need to be mean, and I don't want to make them feel like they have power.

After the attention from her Malala blog posting, Angelina is still blogging and still trying to help other kids feel comfortable with their own uniqueness.

Now that everyone knows about your LD, how does that make you feel?

I wanted to let everyone know that having

a mental or physical disability isn't a bad thing. It's something you have, but it doesn't define you. Don't be afraid to be yourself. Everyone should accept themselves the way they are.

Authenticity!

I guess the way I see it now is that I have a little friend living in my brain and its name is LD. Just like with my real friends, there are good and bad days, but LD has taught me many good things, like not giving up and working hard. It has made me more empathetic and stronger.

How do you comfort yourself on a bad day?

Sometimes I put a lot of pressure on myself. For me, music helps—like playing the piano, singing or simply listening to my favorite songs. I also find Maya Angelou very inspiring. I like her quotes and poetry. My favorite is the one that says "Be a rainbow in someone's cloud." She had a tough life as a child but got through it by doing things she loved, like music, dancing and poetry. I can totally identify with that because I also express myself through music and my writing.

What does confidence mean to you?

The ability to believe in yourself! Don't let anyone tell you that you can't do something. We all have that **superpower** of believing in ourselves, which makes everything possible.

Normal doesn't exist. We should all celebrate our differences, because that's what makes us beautiful!

Does it help you in your day-to-day life?

Definitely. I used to be afraid of letting people know when I didn't get what the teacher was saying because I thought everybody else did. Now I have the courage to raise my hand and say "Can you please repeat that?"

One time recently when I asked the teacher to re-explain something I didn't understand, another kid quietly whispered to me, "thank you."

Just Asking

What's your favorite comfort food
that makes everything better?

Chocolate ice cream

What's the one thing that you
couldn't live without?

My family

If you were an animal, what would you be?

A Yukon Territory wolf

What's the one place you've always wanted
to go—your dream destination?

Elmau, Germany, in the Bavarian Alps

What or who always makes you laugh?

My dad

What do you like to do on a lazy day?

Eat ice cream and watch movies

CHAPTER 22

Celia Suceni Azurdia Sebastian

School. Everyone goes to school, right? From the start of kindergarten, it's pretty much what kids do. Some days it can be fun and exciting, a place where you learn amazing stuff, make art and music, play sports, see your friends, and meet smart teachers. Other days, it can feel so boring and long that weekends can't come fast enough. Still, it's a basic fact of most kids' lives, one they often take for granted.

Except when they can't. Celia, who lives in the village of Los Pajales, Acatenango, in Guatemala, thinks of school as a luxury. Her father struggles to support her and her four siblings, and Celia's first job is to take care of all the housework and her younger sisters. For Celia, this can make going to school almost impossible.

It's like that for many kids in rural Guatemala, especially for girls. There are fourteen boys in middle school for every ten girls, for instance. By the time they grow up, 31 percent of women can't read, compared to about 18 percent of the men. All over the world, in fact, poverty and violence make going to school incredibly difficult, or even impossible. And in many places, girls' education is not as valued as boys', which can make tough situations even worse, leaving girls at a disadvantage for their whole lives.

According to information from the Cooperative for Education, 70 percent of Guatemalans live in poverty and only 10 percent of the population graduates high school.

This is a lot like Yekaba's story from Ethiopia that you read about earlier, but with different circumstances!

Celia sees the challenges for girls because she lives them every day. She says there have been many times when it seems overwhelming and she doubts herself, worries that she isn't good enough, fears that she can't handle it all. But Celia is determined not to be one of those statistics.

"Staying in school is for my own well-being. I couldn't give up because if I did, I couldn't hope for anything better for the future. I wanted to study, I wanted to be better, I wanted to educate myself so I can also make more opportunities for my siblings."

She first started school when she was eight years old. Celia loved it, especially her communication and language classes, gym, and art. Her school was an easy walk from where she lived and it seemed fun. "I only ever thought about studying and everything was good," she remembers.

But when Celia was ten, her life changed forever when something terrible happened. Her mother abandoned her family. Suddenly Celia, her brother, Gudiel, and her sisters, Yessica, Herlinda, and Esmerelda, were motherless.

Celia was devastated. "My mother and father used to fight, but I never thought that my mother would leave. I cried a lot and I lost all of my interest in going to school. But my older sister, Yessica, who was sixteen at the time, helped me a lot. Thanks to God and to Yessica, I finished that year of school."

Things didn't get much easier. After about a year Yessica got married and Celia had to run the whole house. "My dad worked far away and would come home once a month. He would be home for a week and then he would leave again. I don't receive support from him for my schooling because he doesn't make much money, and also because he thinks that I'm going to get married quickly and then all of my schooling will be for nothing."

She cooked all the meals for her whole family: beans with rice, handmade tortillas, and fried noodles, with meat once a week, like fried chicken or chicken stew on Sundays. When her father wasn't working far from home, he was a laborer on a farm on the outskirts of her village. She had to walk several miles each way every day to bring him his meals.

Fortunately, Celia discovered an ally. Her fifth-grade teacher realized that something was wrong. Celia had stopped going out for recess and she was in danger of failing. Her teacher asked her what was happening. Celia told her about how hard it was to take care of everything and everyone at home and do well in school at the same time. As a break from all that pressure, she was using the solitary time at recess for a few stolen moments of quiet.

The teacher told Celia about a scholarship program run by an organization called Cooperative for Education (CoEd) that helps kids like her stay in school, paying for tuition, buying supplies and books, and helping with counselors and mentors.

Celia's teacher encouraged her to apply for the scholarship, telling her that she was smart and strong. And Celia knew that she was on the verge of dropping out if she didn't get support from somewhere. So, even though it seemed like a long shot, she grabbed the opportunity. Her sister Yessica helped her with the paperwork and applications and interviews. And she got the scholarship!

As thrilled as she was to start middle school, the scholarship wasn't a magic wand that erased all her problems. To qualify, she had to pledge to keep up with her grades and homework, not miss school, and study hard. Nothing was just given to her; she knew she had to earn it. And she wanted to, in her heart, but it was super hard.

CONFIDENCE BUILDING BLOCK

Risk!

For one thing, every time she left for school, her five-year-old sister started to cry, which broke Celia's heart. She didn't want anyone to come in and separate her family—she didn't want her sisters to live with other relatives, so she tried not to tell anyone and do it all without any extra help. Still, for months and months, her little sister just kept crying.

Also, all that housework doesn't always fit neatly into a school-day schedule. Here's an example: water is only available on Fridays in her village, so she had to do all the family laundry and bathe her little sisters that day. If that conflicted with a math test, the housework won. If it conflicted with a history paper, housework won. Even with all the help from CoEd, it was hard to keep up. Then her grandmother got sick with kidney problems and Celia took turns with other family members to take care of her, staying up all night with her every few days.

Celia was exhausted and discouraged, and her work in school showed it. She had a lot of absences and her grades were plummeting.

CONFIDENCE QUICKSAND

overthinking!

She was plagued with thoughts that she was disappointing everyone who'd believed in her. "I was scared that I wouldn't be able to continue because I didn't think I was good enough to be able to do it," she told us. "I had thoughts like, 'I'm not cut out for this. I can't do this anymore.'"

So she pulled out of the program and dropped out of school. In some ways, her life got easier. "I wanted to be able to focus on my responsibilities—my grandma, my sisters, and the many household chores. I wanted some sort of break. I didn't have any time for me, and I didn't want another responsibility. Also, I thought that I was capable of handling everything except school, so that's why I let it go."

For a few months, she settled into that new life. Maybe she didn't need school after all, she told herself. Then came a clear shining moment when she realized she'd made a terrible mistake.

"One day, my cousin looked straight into my eyes. She told me to look at her as if she were my mirror. She asked me if I wanted to live like she does, endlessly washing clothes, ironing, making tortillas, working so hard for her family to eat. That was a big motivation. She was right that that would be my future if I don't get an education. I wouldn't be able to change my situation."

Celia did some deep thinking.

"I'm human and I make mistakes, but I will get up and I keep going because it's the only way to survive.

"I had a boyfriend, but I realized that it's not the right time and that's not what I want for me. I would rather be with my younger sisters and help them so they can be happy. I told myself: I HAVE TO KEEP GOING."

CONFIDENCE BUILDING BLOCK

Rebounding!

Putting her fears and regret aside, Celia immediately tracked down a CoEd facilitator in a nearby town and begged for another chance. Her life wasn't set in stone, and she wanted to try to fix it.

This time there were more conditions, like a trial period and requirements for improvements in her grades and attendance. And Celia accepted the challenge.

Did everything work out perfectly after that? Of course not. It's still incredibly hard for her to balance everything at home with her commitment to school. She makes tortillas at night to leave for her family, she cooks nonstop, she does the laundry, and she still feels the familiar sense of responsibility. And on top of all that, she's taken on some work as a maid outside her home, for some additional income. Still, hanging in there, persisting, can be the most powerful weapon she has.

Celia also has a renewed passion for school, having almost let that slip away. She enjoys math, because of the logic and the precision, plus "it's the easiest to study for—it's just a matter of practicing and then you're done." Her goal is to become "a nurse and then a doctor, because that way I can help people that don't have any money to pay for a doctor's appointment."

She understands that school opens her eyes and helps her see beyond her current surroundings in ways even more immediate than her future plans. Education comes from all kinds of unexpected places, not just in a classroom or textbook.

Recently, Celia got to go on a field trip to a park called Xesuj, where she saw animals she'd never seen before, like peacocks, monkeys, and a llama. Another girl lent her a bathing suit so she could jump in the pool for the first time ever, and she got to see a musical performance.

"It was really beautiful because for one day I could enjoy myself like a normal girl without worrying about anything."

JUST Asking

What's your favorite comfort food that makes everything better?

Pepián de pollo (a Guatemalan chicken stew)

What's the one thing that you couldn't live without?

My brothers, sisters, and my dad

If you were an animal, what would you be?

A dove, because it flies high and free

What's the one place you've always wanted to go—your dream destination?

The USA

What or who always makes you laugh?

My seventeen-year-old cousin and my little sisters

What do you like to do on a lazy day?

Go to some green space, lie down on the grass, look at the sky, and feel the wind on my face

CHAPTER 23

Yasmina ali Shaaban

Growing up in a small village called al-Marj, in the Bekaa Valley of Lebanon, Yasmina watched women like her own mother wearing the hijab, a head scarf often worn by Muslim women. When Yasmina looked at her mom, she saw strength, elegance, and the power of faith. She also loved the way the hijab stripped away distractions, making the beauty of her mother's face, of all women's faces, clearer, more emphatic.

But Yasmina knows that this simple act causes controversy all over the world. Some people see girls and women wearing the hijab and think they seem old-fashioned. Others think that the hijab is a symbol of oppression, stopping women from living adventurous lives. Indeed, so many people across so many countries have such strong feelings about the hijab that it can create problems both for Muslim girls and women who choose to wear it and for those who don't. Sometimes it seems with the hijab, girls can't win either way!

In some places, like Iran, hijabs are the law, and wearing them is enforced by police and punishments. In other places, like schools in France or the Netherlands, they are banned. Depending on where you live, there can be a lot of pressure and a lot of criticism.

So many girls from different countries have told us about this struggle that we felt fortunate that Yasmina chose

Girls are taking on this subject in many different ways. One girl is suing an airline for forcing her to remove her hijab to go through security. Some girls fight to get to wear their hijabs in school or professional sports. One girl, Essia, from Tunisia, even created a social media account called Hijab Streetwear to show girls in hijabs living their lives.

to talk to us so honestly about her own experience. It's a complicated subject.

From the time Yasmina was very young, she says that she was entranced with the idea of wearing a hijab.

Yasmina started to talk to her parents about it when she was ten or eleven, but they were worried that she was too young to make that decision.

Yasmina lives in a Muslim village and went to an Islamic grade school, which meant that hijabs never seemed strange to her. But even in Lebanon, a country that's about 60 percent Muslim, many Muslims believe a hijab is too limiting. Plenty of people, including some women in her own family, didn't want her to wear it because it might narrow her options for becoming a professional working woman in the future.

Looking around, both at her community and the wider world, Yasmina realized that there might indeed be some risks. As a student, she was interested in both science and media. She liked to picture herself being a science reporter on TV when she grew up. Except that the TV reporters she saw didn't wear hijabs.

CONFIDENCE
BUILDING
BLOCK

Risk!

In fact, when she paid attention, she could tell that there weren't very many women wearing the hijab in lots of different workplaces.

Maybe when she got older and chose what she wanted to do, the hijab could interfere? But she didn't let that stop her. The hijab felt like a necessary way to express herself and her faith. As she sees it, "the hijab makes girls closer to God."

So she announced to her parents that she was ready and her mom got her a rainbow collection of hijabs. Just a few months shy of turning twelve, she put one on.

"I still remember the first day. It was a school day and I chose a pink hijab. At first, it took some time to fix it and my mom had to help me. But eventually, I got fast. No words can express my pride when I walked into my school wearing it. Four of my friends did it, too. The hijab made me feel safe and strong—a real Muslim girl. My friends and teachers were so happy. I celebrated with my friends and we had cake, sweets, and popcorn. We also got gifts and lots of congratulations."

It wasn't all celebratory, though. As she says, "Some of my family members weren't pleased. They thought I wasn't mature enough and was way too young. My grandma, herself, didn't put on the hijab until she was forty, so she didn't love this idea for me. And then there were other relatives who said, 'You have such beautiful hair, don't cover it!' But, at the same time, my mom and dad were very supportive, as well as some of my cousins."

These days, in her village, Yasmina has noticed that the hijab is becoming less common. Yasmina is also aware of a different stereotype about wearing the hijab: people think that girls are hiding their beauty or not expressing their own personalities. She doesn't see it like that.

She told us, "I try to wear beautiful clothes to show that wearing the hijab doesn't mean you can't dress well or be yourself. I hate wearing tight clothes, so I wear flowing abayas (long dresses) or pants with beautiful colors and fabrics and patterns. I've always loved pretty dresses, and my favorite colors are red and pink. I've got more than fifty hijabs with different designs.

"Wearing the hijab with love, I feel so powerful from the inside that I feel more beautiful and powerful on the outside, too."

In high school, Yasmina wanted to use that power to help people. In her village, there's a shortage of medical care, including eye care. She was sure that she could help, could make a difference. She wanted to work with a nonprofit called Vision Care Association, but people kept saying that nobody would want a girl in a hijab to represent them. Over and over, Yasmina remembers hearing, "The hijab is going to prevent you from achieving your goals."

On top of all that, people didn't believe that a girl should be an outspoken advocate, either. Her reaction? She dug deep inside her own heart and decided, "I will prove the opposite! Just be faithful, trust yourself, and all your dreams will come true."

And that dream did: Yasmina was chosen as a student volunteer supervisor for Vision Care, literally helping people to see more clearly.

But as Yasmina was finishing high school, the stereotyping became more of a barrier.

Yasmina still loved science and medicine, entering science competitions and pushing herself very hard to succeed. She always felt like she was representing her faith in everything she did. Her dream was to become a pharmacist, providing medicine for people in need. She felt like these pieces of herself—her hijab and her determination and her goals—made her unique. And made her strong.

But she was constantly told that it would be easier to just change those dreams rather than pursue them. She shouldn't keep defying expectations. Maybe she should become a teacher, or something else a little more traditional. And people kept pointing to her hijab as the problem, saying it would hold her back. So she'd have to choose: the hijab or the life she wanted to lead.

CONFIDENCE QUICKSAND

Stereotyping!

Yasmina remembers thinking that "my hijab wouldn't prevent me from being a pharmacist, but the medical profession might." What if she went to college to be a pharmacist, but could never work? Maybe it would be better to cave in a little and do something else, like other people wanted. When you face that kind of pressure, it's so easy to fall into that trap of people-pleasing.

Even though her family supported her, Yasmina still felt a little overwhelmed. Then she found another source of strength. "Social media gave me another chance to express myself. It gives equal opportunity to all people. You can see beyond what's right in front of you. You can find people who love you and support you. When they love your content, you can feel the positive energy. And you can use it to motivate others, as well."

She created an inspirational account on Instagram and connected with other girls who were discovering the power of the hijab in their own lives. Focusing on the positive gave Yasmina a chance to step away from negative attitudes and reset her thinking. She was also able to find strength from a far-flung source, the remarkable American icon Helen Keller, who liked to say, "Keep your face to the sunshine and you cannot see a shadow."

And then it hit her: she didn't need to choose just one of the important pieces of herself. She could make them all work together. What if she flipped the equation and adjusted her perspective? Would the hijab hold her *back*? No way. This deeply personal symbol of her faith would propel her *forward*, letting her be her best self. "The hijab is never an obstacle. It gave me the power to remain strong."

Authenticity!

Yasmina thought this through carefully. Figuring out an excellent way to braid these powerful pieces of herself together, she's not backing down on anything.

"Outside my village and region, my hijab could be an obstacle in medical fields, but not if I stay in the Bekaa Valley. There are a lot of Syrian refugees here who prefer to take their wives, moms, and sisters to female Muslim specialists and doctors." So Yasmina is going to college and will emerge as a pharmacist. Maybe that's an unusual, unexpected choice, but it's her choice. She will be that specialist, and she will keep wearing her hijab. For her, it is the absolute right combination.

Yasmina will be able to be her best self, her most authentic self, by knitting her faith, her passion, and her education together. And that's what all girls, wearing the hijab or not, want the right to do!

Just Asking

What's your favorite comfort food
that makes everything better?

Chocolate

What's the one thing that you
couldn't live without?

My parents

If you were an animal, what would you be?

A bird

What's the one place you've always wanted
to go—your dream destination?

Disneyland

What or who always makes you laugh?

My best friend

What do you like to do on a lazy day?

Read a novel

CHAPTER 24

Anna Zhang

Ever since she could hold a crayon, Anna has loved the feeling of creating and being artistic. She didn't think she was amazing at drawing, but her scribbled stick figures were fun to assemble and she could lose herself in her doodles for hours. As Anna says, "When it comes to art, there's no concrete right or wrong; it's very subjective and personal." That's her favorite part—there's no right or wrong. It's not like school. She gets to decide.

When Anna discovered photography, this feeling became even more intense. It helped her get a good look at the world around her and make some sense of it. Anna started sharing her photographs on Instagram, which led to actual work as a photographer, at thirteen years old. Later she founded a magazine while still a teenager.

Finding that thing that motivates you, the thing that you value, can help build confidence and make risk-taking less intimidating. For Anna, that thing is photography. So we asked Anna to tell us about how she uses her passion to fuel her and inspire her to push herself and tackle stuff that scares her.

Anna's Q&A

How did it all start?

I go to China almost every summer with my family, because that's where my parents are from. When we were there, I photographed everything—from flowers at the mall to laundry hanging outside an apartment—to pass the time. Gradually, I took photos whenever I noticed something, not just when I was bored. Like sometimes it was the way the light hit the wall of a building or the color contrast between two vegetables in the supermarket.

Then I just kept doing it when I got home. When I am shooting the chaos of the world around me seems to be distilled. I can pause from the constant go-go-go and take the time to stop, look around, and

This is just what Nati (from earlier in the book) feels when she plays soccer—being in the zone, tuning out distractions, in a state of flow when everything else falls away. A good place to be!

notice the subtle nuances in my surroundings. Photography became a good way to process my thoughts and ideas, to translate what I saw in a fast-paced world into still photos.

Are there things about taking pictures that surprised you? Are there things that other people might not expect?

One of my favorite parts about photographing people is that it pushes me outside my bubble. I've gotten to know a diverse group of people who I wouldn't normally have the opportunity to talk or connect to—like a World War II veteran or a brain tumor survivor or a poet who'd once had a speech impediment. They all taught me little lessons that gave me a bit of a different perspective on the world.

On one of those trips to China, thirteen-year-old Anna began posting her vacation pictures on her brand-new Instagram account, which then blew up. It was totally unexpected, but she decided to just roll with it.

How did your Instagram profile become so huge? How did that transform what you were doing?

I started my Instagram account in sixth grade. It wasn't a business decision. At the time, Instagram was a relatively new platform that was just beginning to become a popular social media app for kids. There was a

Besides building community, here's another way to use social media for good: follow four or five women doing cool things that interest you. Scientists, skateboarders, musicians, activists—it doesn't matter. Seems simple, but it can expand your POV and help you picture possibilities you'd never imagined. Following awesome women can help girls become even more awesome themselves!

budding community of young artists, and it was inspiring to see what people were creating from all around the world. Instagram is very visual, so it was a great way for me to share my work. The whole thing was very organic.

When I got comments on my images or messages from other young artists, I felt like a community was forming that I could be a part of and contribute to.

Then that passion actually turned into something bigger. Seeing her Instagram account and her awesome style, different people and companies asked Anna to take pictures and create content for their accounts or websites.

How did you know what to do next, what steps to take in order to build your business as a photographer?

It was all pretty much new to me. I asked a lot of questions, did a lot of research on these topics, and through trial and error began to find my way. I'd also spend hours on Google, searching online, figuring out marketing terms, or how to use Photoshop, or learning the tools to build a website.

In the beginning, I did a lot of work for trade. Getting products sent to me, to try out or wear, was so fun! My first opportunity came in middle school, so it was such an incredible and surreal experience. I got my first paid job for a small boutique on Etsy. And it made me realize that I could do more with photography than I had ever imagined. It was crazy that something I just enjoyed could earn me some money on the side!

Anna was able to trade her photographs for some of the cool stuff she was shooting!

After that, companies started coming to her for the kinds of images that would appeal to other kids. Including Dunkin' Donuts! As she started to do more of her own photography shoots, often with musicians and artists who were coming into New York, Anna was realizing that the publications for teenagers weren't speaking to her at all. So during the summer before ninth grade, she decided to start a magazine of her own called Pulse Spikes.

Tell us what motivated you. How'd you get this idea?

A lot of the magazines for teenagers centered around celebrity gossip, popularity and fleeting trends, rather than how young people were making an impact in their communities. Feeling uninspired by what I was reading, I was determined to create a platform for youth and by youth, featuring emerging talent and leaders. I named it *Pulse Spikes* because it centered around sharing passions and what gets your heart racing.

CONFIDENCE QUICKSAND

overthinking!

High school was about to start. She had a lot on her mind, getting ready for another new situation. Sometimes, when you are worried about one scary thing, you can disrupt the anxiety by thinking about something else. Anna found focusing on all the little details of starting a magazine kept her mind from spinning out of control and worrying about life in high school. **Dividing things into smaller bite-size morsels also helped.**

How did you cope with starting an ambitious project like this?

The hardest part was how to take a big idea and break it down into actionable goals. At first, I started with what I knew. I was taking pictures at a lot of concerts. So I created a blog for the new magazine and interviewed the artists that I photographed when they came into New York City, which is close to where I live.

After I had posted a couple of stories, people started paying attention and got interested. I officially put out a call for contributors to the magazine itself and explained the concept behind *Pulse Spikes* There is an incredible community of young photographers and writers on Instagram, and I got an amazing response. Of course, that's a very boiled-down summary—most of it was just doing research, trying and failing and listening to what other people had to say.

Of course, we all know that nothing is perfect; nothing rolls along without any bumps in the road. Getting over those bumps is a key to building confidence.

What were some of the hurdles or hiccups when you launched the magazine?

Starting out was difficult. For the first few issues of the magazine, I cold-emailed hundreds of people. Most times, I either got a "no" or no response at all. But as the "nos" built up, I felt like I was getting knocked down and this project was hopeless. It was hard.

I had to shift my thinking. "No" wasn't necessarily the end-all answer. A "no" today doesn't definitely mean "no" tomorrow or "no" in the future. I built on top of the few "yeses" and just kept reaching out to new people. Many of the people who said no at the beginning ended up working with me down the line. You have to be persistent, but respectful.

CONFIDENCE BUILDING BLOCK

Resilience!

Facing rejection is a big obstacle. Were there others?

Another challenge was figuring out the technicalities of the magazine. I spent hours on Google every day, figuring out the little details of the magazine, from the printing and the design of the issues to developing a website. There are so many tiny details that go on behind the scenes, but these small things are important when it comes to bringing the magazine from an abstract idea into a concrete reality.

And sometimes working through a challenge led me to discover a new passion. As I was creating the website, I started to learn a bit of code and realized that I love it. That was outside my comfort zone, but really art and STEM are all part of the same thing. Creative thinking and problem solving.

As Anna worked hard on her dream, she did run into some unexpected reactions.

How did people respond to you tackling your goal with such determination?

CONFIDENCE QUICKSAND

stereotyping!

A lot of adults think that teens are shallow, self-centered, and not old enough to understand anything. Sometimes people don't take me seriously because of my age, but I don't think a number should define who you are and what you are capable of. I hope to show, through the stories we feature, that young people have this immense power to make an impact on a larger scale.

Of course, criticism doesn't just come from other people. Lots of times, the most negative thinking comes from within our own brains, which can totally shut down confidence.

Did you ever feel overwhelmed in the beginning? Did you ever want to just hide under the bed?

All of the time! I tend to overthink things. When I catch myself doing that, I have to remind myself to breathe. I usually try to handle everything alone, to seem like I have everything under control and I can do it all. But that's not true. It's important to ask for help. I also have cheerleaders who support me to continue when things don't feel like they are going right.

Obviously, Anna pushes herself pretty hard to be able to do her photography, the magazine, and her schoolwork on top of it. Now that the magazine has been up and running for a few years, it might seem like Anna's got it going on and never needs to worry again. Sometimes, when we look at other people's lives, they look rosier and better than our own. But in reality, nobody's life is that easy. The perfect life just doesn't exist.

How does it feel now that you've achieved what you set out to do? Is it smooth sailing?

The truth is, there's always going to be something that will make you feel uncomfortable. I tend to want to do everything 110 percent. It can be exhausting and inhibiting.

I can't control or foresee what happens in the future, but I can control how I respond to situations. That is up to me.

I know that I'm going to make mistakes and that everybody makes mistakes. So I'm working on being kinder to myself and recognizing that it's all a learning and growing process.

Just Asking

What's your favorite comfort food
that makes everything better?

Tea

What's the one thing that you
couldn't live without?

My phone

If you were an animal, what would you be?

A puffin

What's the one place you've always wanted
to go—your dream destination?

Iceland

What or who always makes you laugh?

Family and friends

What do you like to do on a lazy day?

Sleep and hang out with friends

CHAPTER 25

Aaron Philip

aron knows that people looking at her might not really see her. They might just see all her challenges, like her cerebral palsy or bulky wheelchair. Or they might notice that she's transgender and doesn't match the box marked "male" on her birth certificate.

Because of the cerebral palsy and what she calls her "spastic arms," Aaron needs a lot of help doing everyday stuff at home and at school. She has to work hard, every minute of every day. It would be understandable for Aaron to do what's easiest, keep it simple, and confine herself to what she knows she can handle. But Aaron realized pretty early on—that's not the life she wanted. She had very big dreams that took her beyond what people expected. And Aaron could only achieve what seemed massively difficult by trying harder than she thought possible, taking risks, sometimes failing, and never ever giving up.

Aaron didn't do everything at once, of course. She knocked down the obstacles like a game of dominoes, one after another after another, building and stockpiling confidence each time. First Aaron used her voice as a disabled kid, tired of being ignored and alone, refusing to be passive. Then as she grew bolder, Aaron used her voice again, declaring her transness and chiseling a new place for herself in the world. And now, in that new place, she's changing the way people think about beauty and physical perfection by becoming a supermodel.

CHAPTER 26

Bella Tipping

Bella is never happier than when she's on a plane, heading off to a new destination. She's from a little country town in New South Wales, Australia, five hours from Sydney. Her first trips with her parents were to a place called the Gold Coast, a hot spot for exciting theme parks, or to the neighboring country of New Zealand. Then they branched out, going even farther around the world, including to Disneyland in California, which became her favorite destination.

Given all her travel experience, Bella had tons of

opportunities to see the way kids tend to be treated in public places and the way most hotels, airlines, and restaurants specialize in adults, rather than thinking about their younger, smaller customers. She developed some strong opinions about it. But she didn't just voice those opinions, she put them into action.

At twelve years old, Bella became one of the youngest business owners in her country when she started **Kidzcationz**, a website where kids themselves can rate all aspects of travel, from service to food, throughout Australia and New Zealand.

Her company has been getting bigger every year, with thousands of registered users from all over the world. It's been so successful that Bella's now thinking of expanding it and creating a kids' travel TV show to go even deeper into a kid's-eye view of vacationing.

Lots of people get frustrated or irritated when travel plans go amok, like when a hotel doesn't live up to its glossy promotional promises or waiters are rude. They rant and complain to their friends or their parents. Not many people get all fired up and then develop a whole new business to solve the problem, like Bella did.

Bella's Q&A

What drove you to start Kidzcationz?

When I was a kid, I'd noticed that hotels supported the adults, but I felt like I was an inconvenience rather than a guest. They don't even think that they need to include kids in that process—even when they're greeting the guests, they just look at the adults.

There was a specific memory that triggered her to take action.

Once on a trip to the US, there was this lovely bowl of apples on the reception desk. Mum was checking in and I remember reaching up to grab an apple. I got glared at so hard that I shrunk back down under the desk because I just felt intimidated and unwelcome.

There were lots of other things. Mum and

Dad would get the luxurious king-sized bed, and I had the little foldout, which was usually dodgy and old and lumpy. Sometimes it would even collapse. The meal options can be unappetizing. Kids want more than just chicken nuggets as meal options. Or pizza.

Pizza and apples. You can never tell what it takes to spark a great idea.

So when I was eleven years old, we came home from an overseas holiday. Mum was putting some reviews on TripAdvisor about the hotels, and I didn't agree with her opinions. I was too young to create my own account, and it frustrated me because I believed they needed to hear what I had to say. Sir Richard Branson (the founder of Virgin Atlantic Airways, among many other businesses) is my personal hero, and I remembered hearing how he approaches an obstacle in life or business—he would say, "Let's do it!"

So rather than setting up an account with

a fake date of birth, I decided to create a platform to allow kids to share their opinion of holiday venues.

That's a pretty ambitious plan, starting your own company at your age. Does that mean that you had always wanted to have a business, to be your own boss?

To be honest, I never had any desire to be an entrepreneur—in fact, I didn't even know what one was! Prior to launching Kidzcationz, I was happy just being a kid.

As an only child, I'd spent a lot of time with adults. I have had a different childhood from most kids. My parents owned a cemetery and crematorium, so I spent a lot of time tending the graves. My job was to throw away the dead flowers on weekends. I guess I was exposed to a lot of grief, but it made me appreciate how short life is and how final death is, so I always want to make each moment count.

Once you knew what you wanted to do, how did you tackle the very first steps?

First I talked to my parents. And I had Mum's help with a lot of it because I was only eleven. I spent a lot of time emailing people and asking hundreds of questions. I can honestly say everyone was so helpful and encouraging. That was just the beginning.

Next there were eighteen months of planning, designing and redesigning before the site was launched. I had many meetings with site developers who wouldn't even speak to me. They just spoke with my mum, and if I interjected, they just ignored me. They were the ones we didn't use!

I'm a shy person and I was tiny, so going into meetings with important people was very intimidating. But I learned that this is my business and so I needed to speak up or I could lose control and the idea I dreamed up would morph into something completely different. Many times, my voice was shaking or I had tears in

CONFIDENCE BUILDING BLOCK

Risk!

my eyes, but I kept going. I also learned that it's OK to ask a question and it's equally OK to hear a no.

My parents financed my business, but they were probably harder to sell to than a bank! I had to provide them with a clear plan of the business and write in an exit strategy. I had to look that up because I had no idea what that even meant.

> An exit strategy is a fancy way of saying a good plan to get out of something if it's not working.

Kidzcationz has really taken off. Bella has had incredible television and radio appearances and international press coverage and interviews. She's obviously created something hugely successful. On the flip side, there have been some unexpected problems.

Nothing ever goes totally smoothly, so can you tell us about the biggest hurdle you've had to confront?

Of course, there were things with the site that caused problems or that we had to work

293

on, but that's normal. The hardest has been something called the tall poppy syndrome, where people in Australia kind of take you down if you get too big. Unfortunately that has happened to me over the years in school. When someone is doing something completely different, it is easier to ridicule or isolate them rather than support them. There will always be someone ready to tear down your self-confidence. It can be very hurtful.

According to urbandictionary.com, tall poppy syndrome is used in Australia to describe the habit of criticizing people who succeed, a.k.a. tall poppies.

But I have learned that it's their lack of understanding or fear that drives their behavior, nothing to do with what I have or haven't done.

CONFIDENCE QUICKSAND

People-pleasing!

We have to stop people from living rent-free in our heads and just do that thing that is burning inside of us.

When this stuff bothers me, though, I usually find my escape in music. I can't sing or play an instrument, but music washes away all my negative feelings. Also puppies, balloons, and flowers make me smile.

Everyone knows that the best kind of travel broadens the way we look at the world. For Bella, it's been an incredible education.

Have you noticed anything in particular that has shaped your worldview?

Yes, absolutely! I was on an international flight and saw a severely disabled man being maneuvered into a seat. He was being dragged around like a lump of meat, treated roughly and kind of manhandled. It was terrible.

Then I researched how people with significant disabilities travel by air and realized nothing had changed for decades. When people with disabilities are lifted into their seats on planes it can be quite dangerous. And I've read a lot of stories about people in wheelchairs or with other physical challenges getting horrible, horrible injuries. I'm Catholic and my faith has taught me to be selfless and to try to look out for other people, so I decided I needed to do something.

I created a Change.org petition to challenge all the major airlines to try to become the world's first "inclusive" airline and allow people to travel in their own wheelchairs. It generated a big response and resulted in me doing some work with Virgin Atlantic (I still haven't met Sir Richard though!). They are putting together an advisory group, so some of us can get together and strategize about how to change the way that people with significant disabilities travel overall.

Through trial and error, Bella has learned some of the key ingredients for confidence, and now she makes sure to fold them into everything she does.

What would you say to another girl who's inspired by an idea and wants to convert it into her own business?

If you have a great idea, find someone to be your mentor. It doesn't have to be someone who has done what you want to do, or even someone who's a successful businessperson. Just find someone who will take the time to listen to your ideas and give you honest feedback. You know more about your idea than anyone else does, but sometimes you can get lost in the details and need someone to bounce things off.

Never give up! As an entrepreneur, once you start one idea, you will find so many more will pop into your head. Work through them all, because one of them is a gem!

Don't expect it to be easy. My site is being transformed regularly and still isn't perfect. And it's always good to have a notepad and pen close to hand.

Never be afraid to push for your business (whether that's advice, support, financing or collaboration).

Never be afraid to hear no. And when you do hear no, don't take it personally.

I have a motto in life:

"If you can think it— you can do it!"

What's your favorite comfort food
that makes everything better?

Pistachio gelato

What's the one thing that you
couldn't live without?

My dog, Frank

If you were an animal, what would you be?

A beagle. They're a loyal, smart, supportive, and goofy
breed of dog, which matches my personality well!

What's the one place you've always wanted
to go—your dream destination?

Iceland to see the northern lights

What or who always makes you laugh?

My dad

What do you like to do on a lazy day?

Listen to music and read

CHAPTER 27

Lan Võ & Linh Đặng

Heading to school? Strolling with a friend? Walking a dog? Rushing to the movies? Whatever it is, girls have the right to feel comfortable and safe walking down the street.

About half the world's population lives in cities now, but they are not always the most comfortable environment for girls. Dealing with inappropriate men or boys who think they have the right to whistle, comment on what you're wearing, or generally say stupid things to you in public is an unfortunate reality. In some cases, this harassment can even be physical and frightening.

We learned all about girls in cities from an in-depth study from Plan International, called *Unsafe in the City: The Everyday Experiences of Girls and Young Women.*

That's when you need to get help. Being safe is essential.

Most of the time, fortunately, it's not a physical threat, but it's an intimidating menace that makes girls self-conscious and tense. And sometimes it can make girls and their parents, especially in conservative cultures, think it's better for them to just stay home. Out of harm's way.

That's exactly what happened to BFFs Lan and Linh. Growing up in Hanoi, the elegant capital of Vietnam, they've been friends since kindergarten. There's so much to do in Hanoi and so many cool places to go. Yet for most of their lives, Lan and Linh weren't able to do any of that.

"We don't feel confident when traveling in public places for fear of being harassed or mugged," they explain. "There is a lack of public spaces that are safe and friendly for girls—who often still face discriminatory attitudes that they shouldn't be active and outdoors as much as boys!"

So, girls like Lan and Linh face a double challenge. Yes, there are hazards in city life. But their families also reacted to that by worrying about girls much more than necessary, which limits their freedom.

When Lan and Linh were little, they both heard, over and over, that the world wasn't safe for girls. That message can take hold in your brain, making it hard for you to leave the comfort and safety of your home.

CONFIDENCE QUICKSAND

Stereotyping!

The problem is that staying inside deprives girls of the opportunities to try new things, have adventures, and take risks—and, yes—build confidence. Using the excuse of safety to keep girls from venturing out will make it hard for them to ever learn to solve problems themselves. They stay in, which makes it scarier to leave, so then they stay in even more—it's a vicious cycle that feeds on itself. It may seem like a comfort zone at first, but it will become a trap.

You can't find confidence shut in the four walls of your home forever.

Lan & Linh's Q&A

What was "home" like for you, growing up in Hanoi?

Lan: I live with my grandparents, uncles, cousins, and my father. My uncle is an officer in the government, so he's the decision maker in my family. My grandparents and uncle are very strict and must be obeyed. When I was little, I ran freely on the streets without any concerns. But my grandmother always thought there were too many dangerous things outside for girls. Immediately after school, she expected me to come home and stay home, be humble and obedient. Hearing this over and over made me believe it.

Linh: Like Lan, I was also born in a traditional family: my mother is a teacher and my father is a driver. When I was a kid, I never went out without them. I only felt safe when my parents or my grandmother were by my side. Deep inside, I wanted to talk and play with other kids, but I hid in my room. My parents tried to get me to come out. But it was confusing because at the same time, they emphasized that I had to be super careful as a girl. Watch every move I made. I had to consider everything I ever wanted to do very carefully—what's positive or what's negative or what's dangerous? I only felt safe to join if things were perfect, which meant that I hardly ever did!

CONFIDENCE QUICKSAND

Perfectionism!

The message that it was both a little menacing and limiting to be a girl was coming through loud and clear. Don't get us wrong, Linh's and Lan's families weren't mean or unkind; they love their girls, but by being over-protective, they weren't actually helping them.

Do you feel like you were treated differently because you are girls? Would boys be treated the same?

Lan: My female cousin, my sister, and I have to do all the chores every day while my male cousin and brother don't have to pay attention to that. All they have to do is study and play. My uncle says that women are caregivers and men are breadwinners. I tried to talk to my grandparents about this, but it's hard to change stereotypes stuck in their minds for such a long time. In my community, boys can go out to play in the evening and then come home late, but only bad girls go out late at night.

Linh: Although my parents love my little brother and me, we aren't treated equally. They think that as a girl, I need to be good at cooking and cleaning, but he doesn't. As Lan said, we have to do the housework, we have to take care of the family. And public places aren't considered safe for girls. Girls shouldn't be too visible because it makes us more vulnerable.

As Lan and Linh got older, they did start to become aware, themselves, that the streets didn't always feel welcoming to them.

What kinds of things did you notice happening around you?

Linh: Many friends of mine were verbally harassed on the street. And people felt like it was the girls' own fault if it happened.

Lan: If my destination was a bit far from home, I'd analyze it carefully from all angles before deciding whether I should go.

By the beginning of high school, though, Lan and Linh both knew that they wanted to make serious changes to get themselves beyond those four walls of home.

What made you realize that you didn't want to be confined by these attitudes or by threatening behavior from men and boys on the street?

Lan: When I was in ninth grade, I got an electric bike.

The farther I went, the more my mind opened.

Linh: I want to go to college eventually, which I can't do from my room! And I learned martial arts to protect myself.

I had to assert myself or I'd be trapped.

Lan and Linh were confused, though, about how to take on the issues of girls' safety and freedom all by themselves. So they got help—found an ally. They heard about a program called Champion of Change, which deals with the issue of safe streets all over the world. They joined it and became local leaders. Lan and Linh got help coming up with great ideas for Hanoi. They lobbied for better lighting for streets and underpasses to make them brighter and safer. They set up meetings and workshops in their schools, and got the girls and boys together to talk through the issues girls face. Even their teachers were interested.

What are you hoping to accomplish by doing all these things?

Lan and Linh: We want those in power to know about the challenges faced by adolescent girls living in big cities. We also want to contribute to building cities that are safer, friendlier, and more beautiful. But we can only help if we are able to participate in city planning and community management and our voices are amplified by those who hold the power.

They loved leading discussions about gender bias and sexual harassment. And they shared their new determination with their families.

What's the biggest lesson you learned as you worked through all of this?

Lan: It's changed the way I look at the world. Now I can talk to my grandmother about stereotypes preventing girls from living the way they want to; I can talk to my uncle and father about stereotypes that also burden men; I can talk to my sister about the stereotypes getting in her way. I know that I'm capable and I have the right to be respected and safe.

Linh: I can have influence. I've learned skills that have helped me look at my own struggle with perfectionism and balance. Trying to be perfect and please others made me uncomfortable because I couldn't be myself and had to say things I didn't believe and behave in ways that I didn't like.

CONFIDENCE QUICKSAND

Perfectionism/ People-Pleasing!

But I'm stronger than that now.

And it taught me that I am most confident when I'm on the stage, either speaking or singing. That's when I have no fear and can just be me.

The girls' work in their community got noticed, and they were invited to be youth ambassadors to the World Urban Forum in Kuala Lumpur, Malaysia. It was a powerful way to test their newfound freedoms, getting to travel to another country and meet an array of other kids from all over the world. And, yes, it was a little bit unnerving.

Lan and Linh spoke in front of rooms full of strangers with their message: **Cities for girls equals cities for all.** Making a city safe for girls means it's safe for everyone. It's a win-win. It was eye-opening to them that girls in cities everywhere face the same issues. And it was thrilling for them to see that girls are taking the lead in solving them, which fired Lan and Linh up even more!

After they returned from the conference, they sensed something had changed. It wasn't that the streets of Hanoi had been fully transformed into completely safe spaces for girls. Of course, despite their hard work on lighting and community education, problems still exist, and they are still smart and cautious on the streets. But what changed was even more important. They're more sure and confident about being themselves out in the world, tackling their own problems. As girls everywhere should get to do!

Resilience!

CONFIDENCE BUILDING BLOCK

After getting out and seeing the world, how does it feel?

Lan: There's definitely a new feeling in my family—they treat me differently because I'm the only one to go abroad for an international event. Now I have more influence both in public, like at the conference, and at home. If someone doubts me, I will not say anything but quietly prove that they are wrong.

Linh: For me, it showed me that my new confidence helps me to help other girls. I like the feeling of speaking in front of people, showing them that I am empowered, that I can be a leader. I want to show girls like me how to be powerful and live the life they want. And if someone doubts me, I will also say nothing. They have the right to doubt. But I am who I am and that makes me strong.

What's your favorite comfort food
that makes everything better?

Lan: Sweet-and-sour pork ribs, fast food
Linh: Many dishes—I like eating

What's the one thing that you
couldn't live without?

Lan: Love and friendship   Linh: Music

If you were an animal, what would you be?

Lan: A dog, because dogs are very loyal!
Linh: A dog, too!

What's the one place you've always wanted
to go—your dream destination?

Lan: The Maldives with my mother
Linh: With my beloveds, I'll travel anywhere

What or who always makes you laugh?

Lan: Family or friends   Linh: It depends!

What do you like to do on a lazy day?

Lan: Dress up and go shopping; cook for my family;
hang out with my friends
Linh: A day free from studying! Wander around
the city, go out to eat with friends, take photos

CHAPTER 28

Jamie Saraí Margolin

Lots of stories are about *doing* something that seems brave or daring. But sometimes, the biggest action in a story doesn't even look like action. It's simply about figuring out who you are and being comfortable with yourself. And that can be a lot harder than it sounds.

It's often one of the most difficult parts of building confidence, like a complicated mystery with a lot of clues. That's how it felt to Jamie. She felt the assumptions coming at her from all over, from parents, teachers, friends, TV, social media, etc. There were so many outside voices trying to pin down her identity that hearing her own voice was almost impossible—until she started to follow the unique threads of her personality, to learn to see them and figure out what makes her *her*.

Some of Jamie's threads seemed tangled to her. She calls herself a "queer mixed-race Latina; daughter of a Colombian immigrant and an Ashkenazi Jew." Growing up in Seattle, Washington, Jamie looked around and didn't see many people like her.

She remembers, "As a kid, it was just confusing. I'm a cross section of many different identities. I'm mixed race. I'm Colombian on my mom's side and Jewish on my dad's side. For a Latina, I'm very light-skinned, which means when I was little, people were always asking me, 'Are you white?' 'Are you a person of color?' 'What are you?' And that's what I was trying to figure out."

CONFIDENCE QUICKSAND

stereotyping!

Even when Jamie was small, her house seemed totally different than her friends' houses. Spanish was her first language. "To us, it's totally 100 percent normal to just be bilingual in the house: it's Spanish to my mom and English to my dad. Back and forth, back and forth. I didn't say a word of English to my mom—that would be the weirdest thing. Or Spanish to my dad. For the first years of my life, my grandma lived with us and helped raise me, which is very typical for Colombian grandmas. Colombian food, the culture, the language: it's all a huge part of my everyday life.

"I call myself half-a-first generation in this country. My dad grew up in the US, but my mom is an immigrant. My mom comes from a poor background and she always reminds me that I get to live like a princess. She's super hardworking, no room for error, no wasting time. She's got that attitude: if you're not going to do something well, don't do it at all, never be mediocre. I grew up with that workaholic mind-set. And she's strict. I'd go to my friends' houses and see how they treated their parents and think—that would never happen at my house!"

On the other hand, Jamie feels equally strongly about her Jewish side. For her, being Jewish is a combination of the traditions and the heritage. "My family from my dad's side is from Eastern Europe, and they're called Ashkenazi. You don't have to believe in God or everything in the Torah to be Jewish. It's also to do with a culture and general way of life. I was raised with the celebrations, going to synagogue and Hebrew school, learning how to read and pronounce Hebrew, having my bat mitzvah, learning about the Jewish diaspora, the Holocaust, and hearing stories from my grandpa about fighting in World War II."

For Jamie, there is another very important thread that makes up her identity: being gay. She didn't fully realize that for a very long time. As she says, "The signs were there since I was little. I remember being seven or eight years old, thinking, 'Oh man, boys are so lucky because they get to date girls and girls are just so much better than boys. But I'm a girl, so I'm going to have to date and marry a guy.' I didn't know that being gay is something you could be. I didn't know that being gay existed. I'd never heard anyone in my family talk about it. I looked at all these Disney movies and fairy tales, books, and movies, but I didn't see anyone like me. I thought, 'Well, this world clearly doesn't want me here. So that can't be me. I have to be something else.'

"Other girls would be talking about crushes

on boys, but I could never picture it for me. I was like, 'ugh.' Still it never occurred to me or my parents that I might be queer. I think part of that is the immigrant culture. I would tell my mom that I didn't have crushes on boys, and she'd say, 'It's because you're more studious and more dedicated than these other girls.' And that's what she always wanted me to be. She always stressed my education, so I believed her. It was a constant refrain in my head, making me feel like an outsider even more."

As Jamie got to middle school, she continued to feel more and more "other" and different. It was starting to dawn on her that she might be a lesbian, but she still fought the feeling. It scared her; it made her feel alone and isolated. Jamie tried to stick to the story she'd come up with in grade school: "I'm not like other girls. I'm just too good to be distracted by that romantic stuff. I'm just not into that stuff." But even as she kept that mantra going in her head, she knew that wasn't true. She remembers that "at the time I was so shrouded in ignorance and guilt that I was just like, 'no.'"

CONFIDENCE QUICKSAND

Fear!

This is like Mena and Zena not seeing Muslim characters like them in the library from earlier in the book!

Still, she looked for characters like her on TV, in movies, in romantic comedies, and didn't find any. And she felt isolated, even unwelcome in the world. At the very beginning of high school, she came up with a compromise in her head. As she told us, "I knew that I was not straight and that I would never marry a man. Period. But for some reason, I decided that even though I know who I am now, I'm going to hide it."

In high school, when some kids were more open about their identity, Jamie started to surround herself with a group of queer friends. She was more comfortable being around people like her. Having a supportive posse can help. She felt that "friendships between queer people are very deep. We travel in packs for safety. It's just refreshing, a relief."

And Jamie discovered some lesbian YouTubers and musicians. Listening to Hayley Kiyoko, an out and proud lesbian singer, and watching her "Girls Like Girls" music video made Jamie feel represented for the first time. As she says, "They made me cry, but they also showed me that a happily-ever-after for a girl like me was possible."

By sophomore year, she couldn't take it anymore. Exhausted by the constant, hounding questions in her brain, "What am I? What is this? I'm so scared. I'm confused," she was ready. First, Jamie told her friends, "I'm gay. There's no hiding from it anymore." Her friends hugged her and told her that they'd always known, of course! She felt so whole, so much more at peace. She thought, "Well, this is me. It's like you're in an oven, and one day you're just ready. The oven bell chimes and you're done cooking, it's time to come out. So I did!"

Now it was time to tell her parents, so that she could begin living openly as her true self. As Jamie remembers, "Even though, literally, the signs were all there that their daughter was the gayest thing alive, they didn't know. So I said to them, 'Hey, I have something I want you to read.' It was a handwritten letter and I put the iPad open next to it. And in the letter I would cue them to watch different video tabs. It was like a

CONFIDENCE BUILDING BLOCK

Risk!

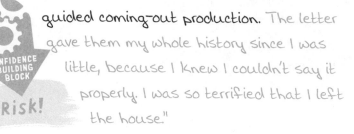

guided coming-out production. The letter gave them my whole history since I was little, because I knew I couldn't say it properly. I was so terrified that I left the house."

Jamie was never worried about the kinds of things that happen to some gay kids, like being shunned, kicked out of her house, or physically hurt. She knew her parents loved her and that she'd always be safe. But she did hope that they'd get it. She hoped that they'd realize, as she had finally done, that this is part of what makes her herself, and not something that would separate her from them, just because it didn't fit with people's expectations.

Her parents responded with kindness. "My dad was just like, 'Why did you have to keep it a secret for so long? You know we love you always.' My mom was also accepting, but still wondered if I really wanted to label myself. I think she kind of hoped it would be a phase. But my only phase was thinking I was straight. She was also a little worried that my life would be harder, that people wouldn't accept me. Maybe I couldn't follow my dream, like going into politics or becoming president. She was just trying to protect me from the world; it came from love.

"But I told her nothing's going to stop me now. I had come to the realization that life is short, and I wasn't going to spend it pretending to be something that I wasn't."

Finally coming out to her parents, to the world, and being authentic gave Jamie confidence in other areas. So she took action on another passion, founding an environmental movement called **Zero Hour** to give kids a voice in the fight against climate change. She'd discovered an essential secret about confidence—it is contagious. Being bold, taking risks, and acting with confidence in one part of her life helped her to build the confidence in another part—those two strands fed each other. Confidence creates more confidence.

"I started Zero Hour the summer before my sophomore year of high school, to make sure that the voices of young people were heard in the battle against climate change. It was exciting," she explains. "We were planning the first Youth Climate March. Taking action for the climate helped me to take even more action for myself.

· "As I became more confident as an activist and a leader, I also started to come out more and more and be more and more open and unashamed of who I am. And I wanted to be that role model for other people, that gay Jewish Latina female representation that I never had. So I'm very very open. By the time I got to Washington, DC, for the climate march in summer 2018, I was very out and I was very proud. It was sick!

"Now I rant on Twitter about the need for queer Disney princesses, alongside my climate

In July 2018, Zero Hour organized a Youth Climate March in Washington, DC. An inclusive collection of kids from all over the country marched! A coalition from Standing Rock Reservation and rapper Xiuhtezcatl Martinez called out the high cost of climate change for indigenous people.

comments. People don't get what it's like to never see yourself represented and to be constantly reminded that you are not welcome or your story doesn't deserve to be told—even though, if the statistics are right, there are millions of gay people whose stories aren't being told."

For Jamie, all the strands of herself have created an incredible whole, someone who can advocate both for herself and for other people. But she knows that it's an ongoing thing to live as your most authentic self. People aren't marble statues, and she's always going to be changing and evolving. And there will always be people, like online bullies, who attack her for all the things that make her unique.

Authenticity!

CONFIDENCE BUILDING BLOCK

In the face of hurtful taunts, Jamie focuses on why she's taking action and why she's sharing her story. "I intend to be the happily-ever-after. The gay president. The person to make things better for other girls like me. This has pushed me to just be brave and be myself."

Her strategy: "Pull a Dory, that fish in

the Pixar movie who never gives up. Just keep swimming, just keep pushing. No fairy is going to come with a magic wand and fix everything for you.

"You just have to swim through the mud until you can swim free!"

Just Asking

What's your favorite comfort food
that makes everything better?

Grandma's empanadas

What's the one thing that you
couldn't live without?

Phone and computer, because that's literally how
I started a movement

If you were an animal, what would you be?

A horse, because horses are majestic and free

What's the one place you've always wanted
to go—your dream destination?

The Amazon rain forest and farming districts
and villages in Colombia

What or who always makes you laugh?

Comedies like *Parks and Recreation*, or my friends

What do you like to do on a lazy day?

Obsessively listen to music, draw, watch shows
with my family

CHAPTER 29

Naomi de la Rosa

All across the world, at some point in their lives, many people leave the place where they were born and move somewhere else. Sometimes they go from small towns to bigger cities. Other times they cross borders to live in another country, to find work, get a better education, or even flee threats against them or violent conflicts. Right now, about a billion migrants are in motion all over the world—more than ever before—in search of better futures. That's a lot of people on the move.

For many, this is a simple process. Whole families go together, and nobody is left behind. For others, it's more complicated: millions of families are splintered, often because of immigration regulations. And for kids, this can be unsettling, even devastating.

When your parents' immigration status is shaky, you can feel like the ground is quicksand beneath your feet. For Naomi, whose parents came to the US from Mexico, this quicksand swallowed her mother and changed her family forever.

This was a confidence challenge like no other, requiring her to tackle things that were hard—with huge consequences for her family—and figure out how to overcome mistakes. Oh, right, and still be true to herself and her own personal goals: success in high school and a college education. Not easy!

Naomi lives in hot, dry Tucson, Arizona. All four of the De La Rosa kids—Naomi; her older brothers, Jim and Bill; and her baby brother, Bobby—are American citizens. Her father, Arsenio, became a citizen long before she was born. Her mom, Gloria, came to the US legally, but her visa expired, so she became what people call "undocumented," without her legal papers.

Gloria went back to Mexico, to the US Consulate General in Ciudad Juárez, which is right across the US border near El Paso, Texas, to admit her mistake to the US immigration authorities and reapply for a visa. As the wife and mother of American citizens, she assumed it would be easy and that she'd be home in time for dinner. She didn't realize there was a law forbidding her from coming back into the United States for ten whole years.

Nine-year-old Naomi and the rest of her family were stunned.

Naomi's Q&A

Your mother was basically deported to Mexico when you were only nine. What was that day like for you?

I remember coming home. I didn't believe my dad when he told me. I searched the house to see if she was hiding or something. It didn't hit me until the next morning when I woke up and searched the house again. She still wasn't there.

I was almost delusional—I decided that she was at her cleaning job at Motel 6. I waited for her to come home at six o'clock sharp. I went outside on the corner so I could see her coming. But she was nowhere. Then I cried and cried.

Since her mom wasn't too far away (she had returned to her hometown of Nogales, which is about an hour from Tucson), they actually did see her sometimes. But even with occasional visits, it was miserable. Naomi's father was much older than her mother and his health had been damaged by years of being a crop duster pilot, spraying pesticides. Her older brothers were in high school and her younger brother was only four.

Obviously, her family changed a lot after her mom was deported.

What was different?

Before my mom got sent away, we had a very contented household, full of love and kindness. But when she left, I felt small and vulnerable. Everything came crashing down. My dad ended up in the hospital with a stroke and a collapsed lung. He had a walker, but it was hard for him to get around. My brothers and I became his nurses.

I also had to be the mom of the house, for my little brother, Bobby. My oldest brother, Jim, graduated from high school and was motivated to join the marines. Then after a couple of years, Bill left for college on the East Coast.

When I was little, I took my family for granted. I didn't know what I had until my mom got deported. For one thing, I didn't realize how hard she worked, which makes me mad at myself now. Because then I saw how much she would do after coming home from long days at Motel 6. I didn't realize all of it until I had to be in her shoes.

Naomi tried to fill those shoes in many ways.

CONFIDENCE QUICKSAND

Fear!

At first, I felt like it was too much and wanted to give up. But I knew I had to make my dad proud with my schoolwork and to make my mom feel secure that I could take care of her baby.

I'd look at Bobby, only four years old. He might have to grow up without my mom physically, but I'd try to be his mom emotionally. And for me, cuddling Bobby to sleep helped me feel safe.

CONFIDENCE BUILDING BLOCK

Resilience!

With your father so frail, and your older brothers starting to move away, how did you know what to do, how to be "mom" before you were even in middle school?

Rebounding!

I like to think you have two options: make mistakes and learn from them, or make the same ones repeatedly and never get anywhere. I had to learn from them or let everyone down. At first, I just had to get up early to make breakfast and get Bobby dressed. Then after my dad got sick, it was everything else.

I'd google recipes and try my best. And I could, at least, call my mom. Still, I messed up a lot.

But I was never afraid to ask questions. Also, I have a supportive community of teachers, academic advisers, mentors, and family, especially my brothers. I was lucky to have my mom's best friend, Letty as my "other

As we talked about in *The Confidence Code for Girls*, friends and mentors can actually change the chemistry in your brain, reducing stress and making you happier and healthier— and more able to handle the kind of confidence challenges Naomi faced.

mother." She helped us out a lot, driving me to the grocery store or on errands. I had a lot of angels to help me.

Naomi had to go through puberty without her mom, figure all that stuff out on her own, in a house full of boys. It was hard. She wasn't able to have much time hanging out with her friends, having sleepovers, or goofing off—basically, being a regular kid. All that on top of missing her mother.

Did that ever make you mad?

I was angry! I blamed other people, definitely. I'd give the border patrol officers the dirtiest looks when we went back and forth. I thought it was all their fault, so I would be rude to them. I didn't know any better.

But after learning about the immigration process, I understood more about what happened. I still hated it, but my resentment toward patrol officers vanished. They're just doing their jobs and following the law, even if I didn't like the outcome.

Were you ever tempted to stay with your mom in Mexico? What kept you here in the US?

Sometimes stuff like this can make you feel like an outsider, like you don't belong here. But I saw this as more like, "I was born here and I have every right to strive and live a prosperous life." Just because my mom wasn't allowed to be here didn't mean I shouldn't be. Actually, it made me realize that I'm empowered and proud to be a US citizen.

Of course, there are lots of advantages to being here. As my father always says, the education! His motto was always "Be number one!" I can't take that for granted. And other stuff. America has free water. In Mexico, you don't get such a basic necessity for free.

As Naomi started high school and her dad's health got worse, her brother Jim returned home from the marines. Still, there was always so much to do: homework, housework, and, as she says, "the nerd stuff I totally love," like student council and robotics.

But she was also drawn to help other kids in the

immigrant community. Helping them with homework at lunch or after school, being there to listen and, most important, to understand and empathize, gave her a way to be the "angel" in their lives, as people were in hers.

Because even with her brother's help, it could be overwhelming.

How did you manage it all and maintain your high GPA?

I make a lot of lists and schedules! Also, it helps to have an overactive imagination and a strange sense of humor. Ever since I was little, I would create scenarios in my head where if I didn't finish doing some task, zombies would eat my family. So if it's late at night and I still have to finish my homework, I'll tell myself that if I don't finish hanging the

CONFIDENCE QUICKSAND

This may have worked for Naomi, but this is a classic case of OVERTHINKING and PERFECTIONISM combined! Use with caution and only in extreme circumstances!

clothes in five minutes, zombies will get everyone. It helped keep me motivated!

Sometimes I use other scare tactics. If I have a presentation for class, I'll tell myself, "Naomi, you have to do this well or you'll get a bad grade, and if you get a bad grade your GPA will decrease, and if your GPA decreases your chance of a scholarship diminishes, and if you don't get a scholarship, you won't go to college, and if you don't go to college you can't help your family or your community . . ."

Whoa, that's a *lot* to put on one presentation or one grade! Nobody's perfect, so why put all that pressure on yourself? What happens when you mess up, as everyone does?

Honestly, I kind of like the pressure that I feel because it pushes me forward. If I do it at my own pace, and not to the point of frying my brain, it works for me.

And I've messed up plenty of times! I procrastinate with schoolwork, which just makes it worse. Sometimes I would forget to give my dad his daily medicine, but luckily my brother would do it if I didn't. I've bombed exams, but since I try to learn from my mistakes, I do better the next time.

Rebounding!

But what happens when, no matter what she does, no matter how hard she works, the quicksand beneath her shifts again? That happened when her father was nearing the end of his life.

When Naomi and her brothers found out their father was dying, being separated from their mother seemed even more unbearable. Her family appealed to the US government for Gloria to come home and be able to nurse him in his last weeks. Their wish was granted. For thirty bittersweet days, the whole family was together. But when he died, her mom had to go back to Mexico. With both parents gone, Naomi could have wallowed in despair.

Except this time, Naomi knows they can make it. Now eighteen years old, she knows that she has love and support, plus remarkable allies and family, so she'll handle it. Naomi's earned a full scholarship to a college near home, so that Bobby can live with her. And her mother's exile will be over in the next year or so.

As she says,

"My life story may seem like a sad one, but it's turned me into a powerful person who can kick butt and do anything."

JUST Asking

What's your favorite comfort food
that makes everything better?

A bowl of chow mein and teriyaki chicken with a
side of cream cheese Rangoon and a pink lemonade

What's the one thing that you
couldn't live without?

My little brother's jokes!

If you were an animal, what would you be?

A cheetah, because it's always so focused

What's the one place you've always wanted
to go—your dream destination?

A cabin in the woods next to a creek, where
it's beautifully green

What or who always makes you laugh?

Eugenio Derbez is my idol!

What do you like to do on a lazy day?

Eat junk food and spend time with my little brother

CHAPTER 30

Zulaikha Patel

It started with her hair. Zulaikha's hair is a glorious explosion of dense, spiraling dark curls, encircling her head in a giant round halo. It's gorgeous and she's always gotten a lot of attention for it. Unfortunately, much of that attention has been hurtful, negative, and even mean.

Zulaikha lives in South Africa, a beautiful country on the southern tip of the African continent. Now a democracy, it used to have an oppressive governmental policy called apartheid, which enforced extreme racial segregation and inequity. The white minority denied many rights and privileges to people of color for close to fifty years. Apartheid was abolished over twenty years ago, in 1994. But Zulaikha, like many black people in her country, feels "you can eradicate the word, but the system still continues to exclude black people." For her, the first inklings of that kind of exclusion came about because of her hair.

Early in elementary school, Zulaikha's hair got her into trouble. Even in a school with mostly black children, there were strict rules about hair length, hair texture, the width of an Afro, and the diameter of braids. The rules might not have called out black kids' hair specifically, but they definitely seemed to be written with straighter, European hair in mind. But Zulaikha didn't tame her hair, letting it be as lush and expansive as it wanted. So she was told that her hair wasn't neat enough, tidy enough, or conservative enough.

Teachers complained that it was distracting to her fellow students, even rude. To her, this message seemed loud and clear: "I was constantly being told that I was wrong, that I was the 'other,' that I didn't fit the standard, that I needed to be fixed."

There were even tests to figure out if a girl's hair was acceptable, like a swimming cap test (would her hair fit under a swim cap?) or a pencil test (if a pencil would stand straight in her hair without falling out, the Afro was too big). Every time Zulaikha underwent these kinds of tests, she felt like her whole self was being judged, not just her hair. "My hair is an expression of my blackness. And asking me to change my hair was asking me to erase my blackness," she told us.

It went straight to the heart of who she felt she was, including her family and her heritage. And she just didn't want to change it, at all.

Zulaikha was an excellent student; she prided herself on her academics. She'd always been determined to prove that she could perform better than the boys. She told us she always pushed herself to be "the top girl, the only girl, and the top black girl." And Zulaikha did get positive attention for her academic success, but as she got older, no matter what, the size of her hair overshadowed everything else she did.

"I was treated like an experiment," she explains. "Everyone wanted to touch my hair, plop their hands in it. Touch my skin. People always asked me what I am. My father is Indian and my mother African, so I wasn't easy to label. I'm not technically 'mixed race' because both my parents are of color. People questioned, why does this girl look black but have a Muslim name?"

It was exhausting to be fighting for the right to be herself, to look like herself, every single day. Zulaikha was forced to change schools just to try to find some peace, but the issue with her hair seemed to follow her wherever she went.

Luckily, Zulaikha could find refuge at home. Her parents were very supportive. As longtime anti-apartheid activists themselves, they could help her identify where this prejudice was coming from and realize that she wasn't doing anything wrong. None of this was her fault.

CONFIDENCE QUICKSAND

stereotyping!

This made sense to her, but she still had to face nonstop comments and threats from teachers and staff at school all the time. Teachers would actually say things like "Who'd expect a top learner to look this way?" or "It's a shame your hair takes away from your achievement."

She remembers the very worst time, which happened in grade school, when a teacher grabbed her hair and said, "You need to cut this *K-word* hair. You look like a sheep." (Except the teacher used the whole word.) For South Africans, the K-word is one of the most offensive words in the world. It's like the N-word in America, and it's actually been illegal since 1976. Traumatized, Zulaikha felt very alone. The bullying became more than she could take.

When it was time to enter middle school, she did something that surprised all her friends and family. She explains, "I felt like I had to conform, so I started chemically straightening my hair. It was miserable. The physical part is unpleasant, the burn, the smell, the pain of combs breaking in your hair. Horrible. And the emotional part was miserable, too. Your hair is your identity. It forms part of who you are, especially African hair. Our hair means a lot

CONFIDENCE QUICKSAND

People-pleasing!

to us. But I was strong-willed. I did not want to hear anything from anybody about it. I kept saying, 'This is the standard. Let me fit the standard. I want to fit in.' And so people accepted it. Actually then I became known for this long, silky, glossy hair. People praised it."

Confusing as it was to be celebrated for being the opposite of her authentic self, Zulaikha was also relieved. She hoped to focus on school, continue to outperform the boys, and then get into a competitive high school. She wanted a time-out from the criticism, but, actually, it showed her that conforming in one way is no protection against being judged in other ways: for being a girl, for being black, for being outspoken. Even without the lightning rod of her hair, she could clearly see the differences between the way boys and girls, blacks and whites, were treated at her school. And she was very vocal about it.

But Zulaikha also got depressed, deeply depressed, and she started to slip in school. The feeling of being overwhelmed, constantly battling but never winning—it all got to her. Her grades dropped and she felt like she was sinking.

Then, at twelve years old, she read something that inspired her and clarified everything she was thinking about. She picked up a book by the famous anti-apartheid activist and hero Steve Biko, *I Write What I Like*, and, as she tells it, "The book grounded me and taught me that history is being made every day. It is being made and can be changed by young people. Chapter for chapter, I discovered something new about my identity, who I could be, who I wanted to be.

"When I finished the book, I made a spur-of-the-moment decision: I decided to cut my hair and go natural. Didn't tell anybody, just did it. All of a sudden, I walk into school with my short, natural, coily, textured hair, and people were shocked. I remember saying to people that I refuse to take part in my oppression. I refuse."

CONFIDENCE BUILDING BLOCK

Rebounding!

The short natural hair and new determination helped Zulaikha crawl out from under that depression and work harder than ever to bring her grades back up. There was a ton of pressure, and she wasn't sure she'd do it. But she did.

When she entered Pretoria High School for Girls, a formal English-speaking school with a majority of white students, thirteen-year-old Zulaikha found the same oppressive rules restricting black girls' hair. The intention may have been to try to minimize difference, but that's not the way it seemed to Zulaikha. These restrictions, again, made her feel that diversity of students wasn't truly being respected or welcomed.

As her hair grew, it got bigger than ever, as did the frequent taunting and harassment from teachers at her school. But this time, there were other girls who agreed with her, other allies. As she says, "There were other people tired of being excluded because of the pigmentation of their skin or the texture of their hair. We were all angry together. We were building up." By then, she'd created enough confidence to know that there was no connection between her hair and her intelligence or her academic performance. She was immune to that argument.

Like at her previous schools, there were pencil and swimming cap tests. Zulaikha was pulled out of class, lectured for hours by herself, given demerits, banned from attending assemblies, and threatened with expulsion. She remembers other girls who were told to flatten their hair with Vaseline.

Then it went beyond the rules about hair. There were other, more extreme measures, like discouraging local African languages among the black girls, but allowing the white girls to speak Afrikaans. Once Zulaikha gave a fiery presentation about feminism as a class project and was ridiculed by her teacher, who refused to give her credit for her work.

Although there are many more languages in South Africa, ten of them are official according to the constitution of South Africa: Ndebele, Northern Sotho, Sotho, Siswati, Tsonga, Tswana, Venda, Xhosa, Zulu, and Afrikaans. Some of these, like Zulu, are more commonly spoken by black people. South African English is also taught in schools and used for official purposes, like in government. At least thirty-five indigenous languages are also spoken, all of which are legally protected by their constitution.

The situation was only getting worse. So she and

some other girls decided to stage a protest during a Spring Day celebration, which was open to the public. About a hundred girls walked silently hand in hand through the school grounds wearing their school uniforms. This time, the school responded with armed guards, who shouted at the girls, threatening to arrest them, trying to intimidate them into walking away. The girls linked arms and refused to move.

Eventually, the girls were corralled into the school. There were more threats, but this time for suspension or expulsion, before they were sent home. As Zulaikha left, she wasn't sure if she'd be back.

But then something unexpected happened. Videos and images of the calm, uniformed schoolgirls facing off against the guards were posted all over Twitter, with the hashtag #StopRacismAtPretoriaGirlsHigh.

Zulaikha and the others did return to school. And a few days later, some government officials came to the school to investigate and hear the girls' stories. It was the first time Zulaikha got to publicly share her experience, which was a huge relief. Also, she felt power from having found allies among the other girls resisting, as she had resisted for so long. The hair policy at her school was suspended, but even better than that, she'd found her voice and learned to use it.

Zulaikha is glad to have taken action, but she also knows changing the rules doesn't change the attitudes behind them. There's still lots of work to be done.

She discovered that this protest ignited something bigger both in other students (protests at schools across South Africa) and in herself. It gave her an empowering sense of community and solidarity. More importantly, she felt free to be her truest self.

CONFIDENCE BUILDING BLOCK

Authenticity!

Her activism might have started with her hair, but now it's expanded. Still in high school, she's a determined feminist, working hard to shift attitudes and improve the lives of women in her country.

In her mind, she's made an enormous shift within herself as well. "Simply living an unapologetic life as a black African girl is activism on its own," she says. "And it's revolutionary."

Her message for young girls everywhere:

"Change has never been a silent or quiet thing. Be loud. Stay loud. Change will be carried out by the young."

JUST Asking

What's your favorite comfort food that makes everything better?

Umngqusho (African corn and bean dish) and stew

What's the one thing that you couldn't live without?

I Write What I Like by Steve Biko, and shea butter for my hair

If you were an animal, what would you be?

An elephant

What's the one place you've always wanted to go—your dream destination?

Masai Mara in Kenya

What or who always makes you laugh?

My best friend, Daisy, and her sarcastic sense of humor

What do you like to do on a lazy day?

Read and write

STICK YOUR PICTURE HERE

CHAPTER 31

Your Story

Acknowledgments

Most important, there would be no book without the incredible cooperation of all these girls. They took time from lunches and homework, from jobs and chores and family, from all the incredible stuff they do, to share their experiences with us. They answered our endless questions, explained their motivations, were honest about their fears and setbacks, and they entrusted us with their stories. Their thoughtfulness and their observations have given us insight into real-life confidence in ways that were both amazing and unexpected. We're honored and privileged! Thank you Aaron, Adelle, the Afghan Dreamers (Fatemah, Kawsar, Lida, Saghar, Somaya, Yasmin), Amika, Anahi, Angelina, Anna, Autumn, Bella, Celia, Ciara-Beth, Dexa, Genesis, Gitanjali, Haven, Jamie, Lan and Linh, Mari, Mena and Zena, Melati and Isabel, Naomi, Natália, Riley, Sam, Taylor, Thandiwe, Yasmina, Yekaba, and Zulaikha.

A huge debt of gratitude to all their parents for

helping with schedules and timing, interviews, translations, photos, and permissions, and for allowing their daughters to share these personal stories, especially: Melina Abdullah, Genelle Butler, Tina Fuentes, Brent Gordon, Mark Margolin, Brenda and Joel Molano, Chris Morrison, Deyar Nasiri, Karyna Pereira, Sarah Patel, Nwiijiaakikwe Peltier, Carla Pritchard, Bharathi Rao, Ali Shaaban, Shelly Shepherd, Bernadette Tipping, Katharina Tropper, and Elvira Wijsen.

Thank you to Emma Watson and Rose Lavelle for lending their voices in celebration and exhortation of these changemaking girls.

Buckets and buckets of thanks to Christy Fletcher, our extraordinary agent who believed in the power of girls from the very beginning of this mission and led the way, fist in the air, so that we could get to do this, and to Alyssa Taylor at Fletcher & Co for her incredible enthusiasm and for managing to keep track of the most minute details with grace and aplomb.

There are many people who helped us in our global detective work to identify and reach these incredible girls. So we offer our most heartfelt and warm thanks to:

Katie Alper, Ketchum

Salma Hasan Ali

Alexandra Andreassen and Amanda Kearney Price, Girl Scouts of the USA

Manuela Andreoni

Juliana Barbassa

Laura Brazee, Kate Ezze, and Tamara Garcia, Plan International

Daniel Donner, Global Strategic Communications Council (GSCC)

Tiffany Drake and Tsebaitu (Tubi) Retta, Global Girls Alliance/Obama Foundation

Cristina Garza, Mission EDC

Tammy Haddad, Haddad Media

Jaime Horn, Andi Foundation

Uma Iyer, National Women's Law Center

Alireza Mehraban, coach and cofounder of Afghan Dreamers

Galen Miller and Trino Schincariol, Packed House Entertainment

Alyse Nelson and Kristin McAvoy, Vital Voices

Illana Raia

Scott Rechler, Learning to Serve

Fish Stark, Peace First

Melissa Winter, chief of staff to Michelle Obama

Luke Windsor, Prosper PR

To Katie Dawson and Howard Lobb, Cooperative for Education; Bernice Morquette, Plan International; Tess Thomas, Malala Fund; and Roya Mahboob, Afghan Citadel Software—special heartfelt thanks for your herculean efforts and monumental generosity.

Heaps of praise and thanks to our intrepid and inventive researchers, June Lei, Cullen Riley-Duffy, and Stephanie Wallace. And to Saanya Ali, for her tireless investigations and creativity, as well as the hours of transcribing wide-ranging, deeply moving, funny, and frequently muffled audio interviews.

Enormous gratitude to our editor Claudia Gabel at Harper for recognizing that telling these stories was the next step for *The Confidence Code for Girls* and becoming such a fervent champion. To the unsinkable Camille Kellogg, for her eagle eye and indefatigable spirit. To Stephanie Guerdan, for never missing a beat. To the brilliant art department and Alison Donalty and Alison Klapthor, and to all the other talented folks at Harper supporting this book and getting these stories out into the world: Barb Fitzsimmons, Caitlin Lonning, Alexandra Rakaczki, Josh Weiss, Kim Stella, Nicole

Moulaison, Vaishali Nayak, Victor Hendrickson, and Cindy Hamilton.

Big shout-out to the amazing and creative folks at Stonesong for making the book look as distinctive and compelling as the girls themselves: Alison Fargis, Ellen Scordato, and Joey Cavalier. To Jessica Nordskog, for her lively and engaging chapter openers, and Julie Lerche, who captured Aaron, the Afghan Dreamers, Greta, and Nati in stunning graphic form, thank you!

And of course, to our families:

Katty: To Poppy, Jude, Maya, and Felix. I am so lucky to be your mum and to have your love and support and humor. My best moments are always the ones I spend with you. To Tom: thank you, for everything—for Senegal and Washington and all our adventures in between. It's all more fun with you.

Claire: Della, you are the wisest, most insightful fourteen-year-old—or whatever-year-old—I know, and you are always my intrepid confidence Sherpa. Hugo, you make me laugh, hug me when I'm overwhelmed, and also help me constantly witness in you what the confidence gold standard might be; and Jay, I could never do this without your love and support.

JillEllyn: To Cullen and Eoin, my moptops, for tea and snack deliveries, rapt interest in all these tales, mostly patient tech support, boundless good nature, and wry humor. Mostly, for just being the you-est of you. To Duff, for every single shiny thing, forever. As always, for Miles.

Last, we want to celebrate and thank each other. As we say over and over, find your allies and make sure you have a posse—we've done just that! We want to take a page from our own research and tout all the fun we had telling these stories and the joy of working together. To Katty, Claire, and JillEllyn, from Katty, Claire, and JillEllyn, thank you for the pleasure of this project!

Shout-outs: Sources & References

Here's more information about some of the subjects and issues that came up in the girls' stories. There's a vast world of knowledge out there, but check out these places to start!

Chapter 1: *Melati & Isabel*

Bye Bye Plastic Bags: *To find out more about Melati and Isabel's movement: www.byebyeplasticbags.org*

Oceanic Society: *To learn seven easy ways you can help reduce plastic in the ocean: www.oceanicsociety.org/blog/1720/7-ways-to-reduce-ocean-plastic-pollution-today*

Plastic Pollution Coalition: *To learn more about plastic packaging and the planet: www.plasticpollutioncoalition.org*

Chapter 2: *Riley*

National Girls & Women in Sports Day: *For more info on confidence through sports and physical activity: ngwsd.org*

Women's Sports Foundation: *To learn more about the fight for equal pay in women's sports: www.womenssportsfoundation.org/education/ fight-equal-pay-womens-sports*

Chapter 3: *Mari*

Dear Flint Kids Project: *Mari started a letter project that allows people from all over the world to write supportive letters to kids living in her community. You can write your own letter and address it to: Mari Copeny PO Box 138 Flint, MI 48501*

Clean Water Act: *To find out more about lead in drinking water across the country and strengthening water protections: www.cleanwateraction.org*

Charity: Water: *To learn more about clean water conditions worldwide: www.charitywater.org/ global-water-crisis*

Chapter 4: *Ciara-Beth*

Autistic Self Advocacy Network: *To discover more activities and games that focus on communication and social skills for children with autism: autisticadvocacy.org*

Autism Highway: *For more information on autism-related events and fun, interactive games for kids with autism: autismhwy.com*

Chapter 5: *Haven*

International Paralympic Committee: *For more information on the Paralympic Games and Para athletes: www.paralympic.org*

National Center on Health, Physical Activity and Disability: *To find out more about the health benefits of physical activities and sports programs for children with different abilities: www.nchpad.org*

Chapter 6: *Afghan Dreamers*

Digital Citizen Fund: *To learn more about educational programs and IT opportunities for women and children in developing countries: digitalcitizenfund.org*

Code to Inspire: *For more information on female*

students in Afghanistan training in technology and coding: www.codetoinspire.org

UNICEF: *For more information about girls' education in Afghanistan, including the statistics: www.unicef .org/afghanistan/education*

Chapter 7: *Yekaba*

Plan International: *To find more information about global educational challenges: plan-international.org/ quality-education*

Girls Advocacy Alliance: *To learn more about initiatives by girls to combat gender-based violence and discrimination: defenceforchildren.org/ girls-advocacy-alliance*

Chapter 8: *Amika*

Free Periods: *For more information about Amika's organization: www.freeperiods.org*

The Pink Protest: *For more information about period empowerment: www.pinkprotest.org*

Women Strong International: Empowering the Period: *To learn more about access to menstrual and reproductive health education, sanitary pads, and*

school toilets across the world: www.womenstrong
.org/topics/womens-health

The Trevor Project: *For additional information on period concerns for the transgender and nonbinary community, check out: www.thetrevorproject.org/ trvr_support_center/trans-gender-identity*

Callen-Lorde: *To learn more about transgender menstrual health and services available, go to: callen-lorde.org/transhealth*

Chapter 9: *Sam*

Utah Girls Tackle Football: *For more information about the league Sam founded: www.utahgirlstacklefootball. com*

Women Sport International: *To learn more about research-based advocacy for women in sports: womensportinternational.org*

Women's Football Alliance: *To learn more about women's tackle football across the United States and around the world: www.wfaprofootball.com*

Chapter 10: *Taylor*

Girl Scouts: *To learn more about the adventures and*

opportunities in Girl Scouts: www.girlscouts.org

In Her Shoes: *To read about girls' freedom of expression and pursuit of creativity: www.inhershoesmvmt.org/ mission*

Chapter 11: *Genesis*

USGS: Science for a Changing World: *To learn about how much water it takes to produce a hamburger: water. usgs.gov/edu/activity-watercontent.php*

Farm Sanctuary: *For more information on saving farm animals: www.farmsanctuary.org*

Million Dollar Vegan Campaign: *To learn more about the relationship between diet and the planet: www.milliondollarvegan.com*

Chapter 12: *Greta*

United Nations Special Report: Global Warming: *To see the climate report by scientists that Greta submitted to the US Congress: www.ipcc.ch/sr15*

National Geographic Kids: *To learn more facts about climate change and ecosystems: www.natgeokids .com/uk/discover/geography/general-geography/ what-is-climate-change*

World Nomads: *For tips on environmentally*

friendly travel: www.worldnomads.com/
responsible-travel/make-a-difference/planet/
top-10-tips-for-environmentally-friendly-travel

Chapter 13: *Mena & Zena*

Girls of the Crescent: *To more find books and resources from Mena and Zena: www.girlsofthecrescent.org*

Muslim Women's Organization: *To discover more about Muslim women's advocacy: www.mwo-orlando.org/empowerment*

WISE Muslim Women: *To learn more about Muslim women leaders around the globe: www.wisemuslimwomen.org/about*

Chapter 14: *Adelle*

Adelle's Creperie: *For more information about Adelle's tasty menu: www.adellescreperie.com/*

Move for Hunger: *For more information about the fight to eradicate the food deserts across the United States: www.moveforhunger.org/harsh-reality-food-deserts-america/*

Teen Business: *To read more about teens starting businesses and the resources for them: www.teenbusiness.com/*

Chapter 15: *Anahi*

Clothes to Kids: *To discover how donating clothes to low-income children can change their lives: clothestokids.org*

Operation Warm: *To learn more about the impact of schoolchildren needing warm clothes, go to: www.operationwarm.org*

Chapter 16: *Thandiwe*

National Education Association Educational Justice: *To learn more about the movement for racial equity in education: neaedjustice.org*

LA Students Deserve: *To discover how students in LA are preparing themselves with the necessary skills for life after school: www.schoolslastudentsdeserve.com*

Chapter 17: *Dexa*

Days for Girls International: *To discover how girls' lives are transformed through access to sustainable menstrual care: www.daysforgirls.org*

Because I Am a Girl: *To check out the life-changing initiatives and programs launched by girls all over the world: plan-international.org/because-i-am-a-girl*

Chapter 18: *Autumn*

Mother Earth Water Walk: *To learn more about Autumn's aunt Josephine and the Mother Earth Water Walkers: www.motherearthwaterwalk.com*

World Water Council: *For more information on the fight for water security and sustainability: www.worldwatercouncil.org/en*

Chapter 19: *Natália*

Goals for Girls: *To discover how soccer is being used to teach young women life skills: www.goalsforgirls.org*

Soccer without Borders: *For more information on the power of soccer to create change and bring people together: www.soccerwithoutborders.org*

Chapter 20: *Gitanjali*

Girls Are Awesome: *To discover how female entrepreneurs are making a difference with their inventions: girlsareawesome.com/ five-female-inventors-know*

Coalition to Prevent Lead Poisoning: *To learn more about the fight to combat lead in our water: theleadcoalition.org*

Chapter 21: *Angelina*

Care Gift Elves: *For information about Angelina's kindness initiative: www.thecaregiftelves.com*

Smart Kids with Learning Disabilities: *To discover how kids with learning disabilities can tap into their strengths, gifts, and talents: www.smartkidswithld.org*

Malala Foundation: *For inspiration on girls all over the world fighting for education: www.malala.org*

Chapter 22: *Celia*

Cooperative for Education: *To read about how CoEd is helping children break the cycle of poverty through education: coeduc.org*

Global Girls Alliance: *For more information about expanding girls' education around the world: www.obama.org/girlsopportunityalliance*

Chapter 23: *Yasmina*

Facing History: *To learn more about the history of the hijab throughout the world: www.facinghistory.org/civic-dilemmas/brief-history-veil-islam*

World Hijab Day: *For stories about the hijab in women's lives: worldhijabday.com/about-us*

Kids and Race: *To read more facts about the hijab:*

www.kidsandrace.org/blog/2019/1/31/8-facts-about-muslim-headscarves-for-world-hijab-day

Chapter 24: *Anna*

Pulse Spikes: *To see Anna's magazine: pulsespikes.com*

The Art Gorgeous: *To discover how women are blazing trails in art and fashion: www.theartgorgeous.com*

Chapter 25: *Aaron*

Cerebral Palsy: *For information on how kids with cerebral palsy embrace opportunities: www.cerebralpalsy.org/inspiration/opportunities*

It Gets Better: *To read more about LGBTQ youth: itgetsbetter.org*

Chapter 26: *Bella*

Kidzcationz: *To discover tips, travel ideas, and vacation planning for kids from the website that Bella created: kidzcationz.com*

Easy Access Travel: *For information on how people with disabilities vacation: easyaccesstravel.com*

Chapter 27: *Lan & Linh*

Gals Forum International: *To discover more projects*

focused on making cities safe for adolescent girls and women: galsforum.org/category/programs/safer-cities-for-adolescent-girls

Champions of Change for Gender Equality and Girls' Rights: *For more information on advancing gender equality and fighting against gender discrimination: plan-international.org/youth-activism/champions-change*

Chapter 28: *Jamie*

Zero Hour: *For more information on the environmental justice organization Jamie founded: thisiszerohour.org/*

The Climate Change Reality Project: *To learn about how to get involved in climate change advocacy in your city: www.climaterealityproject.org*

GLSEN: *To discover more about the fight for LGBTQ issues in K–12 education and the movement to create a safe and affirming learning environment for LGBTQ students: www.glsen.org*

Chapter 29: *Naomi*

American Immigration Council: *For more information on the fight to keep families together: www.americanimmigrationcouncil.org*

Hispanic Federation: *To learn more about the contribution of Hispanic families and institutions across the country: hispanicfederation.org*

Chapter 30: *Zulaikha*

Make Every Woman Count: *To discover how African women are fighting to strengthen the voice, impact, and influence of African women's rights: www.makeeverywomancount.org*

18twenty8: *For more information on how South African girls are using higher education as a tool for their empowerment: www.18twenty8.org*

Photo credits

Chapter 1: Melati & Isabel Wijsen
Photo credit: Bye Bye Plastic Bags

Chapter 2: Riley Morrison
Photo credit: Chris Morrison

Chapter 3: Mari Copeny
Photo credit: Loui Brezzel

Chapter 4: Ciara-Beth Griffin
Photo credit: Geraldine Griffin

Chapter 5: Haven Shepherd
Photo credit: Deisy Mendoza, Water and Grace
Photography

Chapter 7: Yekaba Abimbola
Photo credit: Plan International

Chapter 8: Amika George
Photo credit: The Pink Protest

Chapter 9: Sam Gordon
Photo credit: Larry Gordon

Chapter 10: Taylor Fuentes
Photo credit: Tina Fuentes

Chapter 11: Genesis Butler
Photo credit: Pollution Studios

Chapter 13: Mena & Zena Nasiri
Photo credit: Deyar Nasiri

Chapter 14: Adelle Pritchard
Photo credit: Carla Pritchard

Chapter 15: Anahi Molano
Photo credit: Brenda Molano

Chapter 16: Thandiwe Abdullah
Photo credit: Leroy Hamilton

Chapter 17: Dexa
Photo credit: Plan International

Chapter 18: Autumn Peltier
Photo credit: Linda Roy, Ireva Photography

Chapter 20: Gitanjali Rao
Photo credit: Bharathi Rao

Chapter 21: Angelina Tropper
Photo credit: Angelina Tropper

Chapter 22: Celia Suceni Azurdia Sebastian
Photo credit: Cooperative for Education

Chapter 23: Yasmina ali Shaaban
Photo credit: Nadia Kenaan

Chapter 24: Anna Zhang
Photo credit: Anna Zhang

Chapter 26: Bella Tipping
Photo credit: Bernadette Tipping

Chapter 27: Lan Võ & Linh Đặng
Photo credit: Plan International

Chapter 28: Jamie Saraí Margolin
Photo credit: Jamie Saraí Margolin

Chapter 29: Naomi de la Rosa
Photo credit: Naomi de la Rosa

Chapter 30: Zulaikha Patel
Photo credit: Tinani Chikura, Wits Junction

Author Photos:
Katty Kay: Felix Mallaby-Kay
Claire Shipman: Marissa Rauch
JillEllyn Riley: Kathy Nicolosi

About the Authors

KATTY KAY, CLAIRE SHIPMAN, and JILLELLYN RILEY are the bestselling authors of *The Confidence Code for Girls* and *The Confidence Code for Girls Journal*. Katty and Claire, longtime friends, have been writing books together for over a decade. They've also cowritten the *New York Times* bestsellers *Womenomics* and *The Confidence Code*. JillEllyn joined them to help create the Confidence Code for Girls books.

KATTY KAY is the anchor of BBC World News America, based in Washington, DC. She is also a frequent contributor to *Meet the Press* and *Morning Joe* and a regular guest host of *The Diane Rehm Show* on NPR. In addition to her work on women's issues, Katty has covered the Clinton administration; four presidential elections; and the wars in Kosovo, Afghanistan, and Iraq. She was at the Pentagon just twenty minutes after a hijacked plane flew into the building on 9/11—one of her most vivid journalistic memories is of interviewing soldiers still visibly shaking from the attack. Katty grew up all over the Middle East, where her father was posted as a British diplomat. She studied modern languages at Oxford and is a fluent French and Italian speaker with some "rusty Japanese." Katty juggles her journalism with raising four children with her husband, a consultant.

CLAIRE SHIPMAN is a journalist, author, and public speaker. Before turning to writing, Claire spent fourteen years as a regular contributor to *Good Morning America* and other national broadcasts for ABC News. Prior to that, she served as the White House correspondent for NBC News. She also worked for CNN for a decade, covering the White House, and was posted in Moscow for five years. She'll never forget the fall of the Soviet Union and watching ordinary citizens swarm city squares to pull down, with rope and a lot of anger, gigantic statues of the unpopular communist leaders. Her coverage helped CNN earn a Peabody Award. She also received a DuPont Award and an Emmy Award for coverage of the 1989 Tiananmen Square student uprising. She studied Russian at Columbia University and also earned a master's degree from the School of International Affairs there. She's now a member of Columbia's board of trustees. She lives in Washington, DC, with her husband, son, daughter, and a pack of dogs.

JILLELLYN RILEY is a writer and editor with extensive experience in crafting and telling stories. She's worked with bestselling, innovative children's authors, as well as on nonfiction and fiction for adults. Her cowritten middle grade series is the Saturday Cooking Club. JillEllyn lives in Brooklyn, New York, with her husband, two sons, and canine ally, Stella.

From *New York Times* bestselling authors

KATTY KAY, CLAIRE SHIPMAN
and JILLELLYN RILEY

Embrace the confidence code
and become a girl of action!

HARPER

An Imprint of HarperCollinsPublishers

www.harpercollinschildrens.com